Great Taste
No Gluten

Sherry Brescia

All materials in Great Taste No Gluten are intended to describe an approach to healthy living that has had positive effects for the many thousands of people who have implemented its principles.

Nothing in Great Taste No Gluten is intended to constitute medical treatment or advice of any nature. Moreover, as every person responds differently to diet and lifestyle changes, it is strongly recommended that any person desiring to make modifications to his or her diet or lifestyle consult with his or her physician or medical practitioner.

It is not intended as a replacement for medical treatment. No medical claims are intended express or implied. No statements made in the application or related documentation have been evaluated by the U.S. Food and Drug Administration. Nothing contained in the materials is intended to diagnose, treat, cure or prevent any disease.

The buyer of Great Taste No Gluten assumes all risks in using the system, waving any claims against Sherry Brescia, Sharon Brescia, Holistic Blends, Inc. and its affiliates for any and all mental or physical injuries. This includes all information acted upon from complimentary or paid newsletter content. The buyer/user also agrees to assume liabilities when other persons have access to Great Taste No Gluten whether for commercial or private use.

In no case will Sherry Brescia, Sharon Brescia, Holistic Blends, Inc. and its affiliates or other distributors of Great Taste No Gluten be liable for chance, accidental, special, direct or indirect damages resulting from use, misuse or defect of its manuals, instructions or documentation.

*This book is dedicated to my children, Danielle and Mickey.
You are the lights of my life and inspire me
to help make this world a better, healthier place.
Love you both with all my heart.
-Mom*

*Plus special thanks to my staff for their enthusiastic taste-testing and critiquing of
our gluten-free creations over the last several months, and especially to Linda Hunter,
who spent tireless hours shopping and preparing many of the delicious recipes
that have become a part of this book. You're all the best!*

Introduction

The late, great Erma Bombeck once said, "I am not a glutton — I am an explorer of food."

She and I have a lot in common, although we both "explore food" for different reasons. Her reason appeared to be strictly for her taste buds while mine has to do with the *rest* of the body. But I wasn't always that way—quite the opposite actually. You see I LOVE food. Always have. From the time I was a kid to my late 20's I was more of a person that "lived to eat" instead of "eating to live."

But I suffered. Throughout my childhood and teen years, I experienced terrible stomach pain after I ate. It was sporadic, so I never saw a connection between my symptoms and any specific *kind* of food.

As I got older my symptoms escalated to the point where they prevented me from dining out and socializing with friends. I finally hit my digestive "brick wall" at age 28 when I was hospitalized for a week. The result? I was told I had IBS (irritable bowel syndrome) and given prescription medication. Problem was, the drugs only made me tired and did nothing for my gas, bloating and pain. I was miserable and felt hopeless.

But I received an answer to my prayers of desperation when I learned how to properly combine my foods so that it allowed my body to efficiently digest what I've eaten. Once I began eating this way, my symptoms disappeared *completely*, never to return. I have since been completely free of IBS for nearly 20 years and have helped tens of thousands of others to alleviate digestive disorders by educating them on the principles with my Great Taste No Pain program. http://www.greattastenopain.com

There has, however, been one persistent "antagonist" in this happy story. That antagonist has prevented even my most dedicated followers from feeling as good as they can possibly feel.

It's called *gluten*. Gluten is a protein found in wheat, barley and rye. It's what makes dough sticky and gives bread that moist, chewy, tender texture that is <u>so</u> irresistible. It's also what makes people with celiac disease and gluten sensitivity very, *very* sick.

Gluten sensitivity can wear many faces. In addition to the typical GI symptoms (cramps, gas, bloating, constipation, diarrhea) people with the condition can also suffer from depression, skin problems, fatigue, joint pain, muscle pain, mouth sores, underweight, malnourishment and nutritional deficiencies.

Since vague symptoms like these are also seen with many other illnesses, the typical gluten-sensitive person can go as long as *10 years or more* before being properly diagnosed and treated!

Once gluten sensitivity is identified, the standard treatment appears easy: Avoid gluten. However it's not that simple. First, because gluten is practically everywhere. And second, even if a gluten-sensitive person avoids gluten 100%, if they improperly combine their foods, they will likely continue to suffer digestive problems and never know why. So, I found another important crusade to pursue. Because even the most astute food combiner will be sick as a dog if they are gluten-sensitive and eat gluten.

So out of necessity, Great Taste No Gluten was born. It's the only program ever developed that pairs proper food combination principles with delicious gluten-free recipes.

On one hand, most real foods in their natural state are inherently gluten-free (such as meats, vegetables, fruits, dairy products and certain grains), so that part was easy. The challenge was creating delicious alternatives for those foods that rely *heavily* on gluten—like breads, cakes, muffins, pancakes, pie crust and crackers. For anyone who has ever tried to go gluten-free, they know, nearly all of the boxed mixes and prepackaged gluten-free foods have terrible textures and the tastes are even worse.

This soon became a vast undertaking with nearly two years of research, and recipes being created, tested, modified and retested. I involved my entire staff in the process, having them sample and rate our creations. I am confident you'll be pleased with the results of our hard work because every recipe in this book is positively mouth-watering.

For those of you who are celiac or gluten sensitive, your dreams have come true—you are about to enjoy many new incredibly delicious gluten-free dishes. And for those of you who have continued to suffer because you were unknowingly eating the wrong foods together, the Great Taste No Gluten manuals will give you the final piece to your pain-free life puzzle.

Enjoy your new, wonderful gluten-free life.

Sherry Brescia

Table of Contents

# Breads and Breakfast Items

Breakfast Frittata   **Category: C**   **Serves: 2-3**

6 large eggs (preferably organic brown eggs)
1/3 cup milk or half-and-half
1/2 cup crumbled Feta cheese
1/2 of a red bell pepper, diced
1/2 of a green bell pepper, diced
1/4 cup diced onion
1 cup broccoli florets, steamed until tender
1/2 cup white or baby Bella mushrooms, sliced
1/4 cup sliced gluten-free black olives
Olive oil
Salt and pepper to taste
2 tablespoons grated Parmesan or Romano cheese for topping

Prepare all vegetables and have them ready.

In a deep mixing bowl, beat together eggs and milk or half-and-half. Stir in Feta cheese.

Coat the bottom of a 10 inch skillet with olive oil and heat over medium heat. Add peppers and onions and sauté until they soften, about 5 minutes. Add broccoli, mushrooms and olives and sauté another 3 minutes.

Pour egg mixture evenly on to vegetables and cook, lifting up cooked egg around edge occasionally to let raw egg flow underneath, for about 3 minutes. Reduce heat to low and cook until underside is golden, about another 5 minutes.

The next step is up to you. If you want a "picture perfect" frittata, slide the frittata onto a plate, invert the pan onto the plate (using oven mitts) and flip the frittata back over into the skillet. Or, if you don't care about being neat, break the frittata up into 5-6 manageable pieces with a spatula and flip them over individually in the pan. Continue cooking over low heat until the underside is golden, about 5 minutes. Sprinkle with Parmesan or Romano cheese and serve.

Variations:
- Substitute pitted gluten-free Kalamata olives for black olives
- Use whatever vegetables are your favorites-spinach, zucchini and escarole all work well
- Use shredded Cheddar or Swiss cheese in place of the Feta

Serve with:
Category A items of your choice

Pancakes   **Category: B**   **Serves: 8–10**

2 eggs
3/4 cup rice flour
1 tablespoon baking powder
1/4 cup oil
1/4 teaspoon salt
2 tablespoons Xanthan gum
1/2 teaspoon vanilla extract
1 cup milk

Place all the ingredients in medium bowl, adding the milk last. Mix very well. The batter will become thick. Heat a pan or griddle to medium heat. Pour the batter in the pan to the desired size of pancake. Cook until small bubbles appear on the surface and the bottom is lightly browned. Flip and continue to cook until lightly browned on both sides.

Serve with:
Butter, maple syrup and jelly
Category A items of your choice

Waffles   **Category: B**   **Serves: 4**

3 eggs
1 1/3 cups rice flour
1 tablespoon baking powder
1/3 cup oil
1/4 teaspoon salt
2 tablespoons sugar
1 cup milk
1 teaspoon Xanthan gum
1/2 teaspoon vanilla extract

Preheat waffle iron.

Place all the ingredients in a medium bowl. Mix well. The batter will be very thick. It will become thicker as it sits. Place 1/2 cup of batter into the waffle iron. Cook to your desired level of browning, about 1 1/2-2 minutes.

Serve with:
Butter, maple syrup and jelly
Category A items of your choice

Breakfast Smoothies   **Category: Fruit**   **Serves: 2-3**

4 cups fresh fruit of your choice
1 large banana
1 cup fruit juice of your choice
1 cup ice cubes

Put all ingredients into a blender; blend on high speed 1 minute until smooth and thoroughly mixed. If mixture is too thick, add fruit juice to desired consistency.

Great fresh fruit and juice combinations include:

- Mixed berries-strawberries, blueberries, and raspberries with berry juice.
- Peaches, mangos, nectarines and pineapple with orange or pineapple juice
- Mixed melons-watermelon, cantaloupe and honeydew with mixed fruit juice
- Apples, pears and grapes with apple or cran-apple juice

Serve with:
These are made from fresh fruit, so they cannot be combined with any other food (except more fruit). They can be the first course of a larger breakfast or dinner, but wait 20 minutes for the smoothie to pass through the stomach before other foods are eaten.

Cinnamon Coffee Cake   **Category: B**   **Serves: 9**

1/4 cup butter
1/2 cup sugar
2 eggs
1 egg white
1/2 cup plain yogurt
3/4 cup rice flour
1 tablespoon baking powder
1 teaspoon baking soda
1/2 teaspoon salt
1 teaspoon vanilla extract
3/4 teaspoon Xanthan gum
2 teaspoons apple cider vinegar

Topping:
1/2 teaspoon ground cinnamon
1/4 cup brown sugar
3 tablespoons butter

Preheat oven to 350°. Lightly grease a 9 inch round or square baking pan.

Combine butter with sugar in a medium sized bowl. Add eggs and egg white. Beat with an electric mixer until light yellow and a little thicker. Add all remaining ingredients except the topping. Spread in the baking pan.

Mix all the topping ingredients together until crumbly. Sprinkle evenly on top of the dough.

Bake for 25-35 minutes, or until a toothpick inserted in the middle comes out clean.

Serve with:
Sweet breads are best eaten alone for breakfast or as a dessert. (See guidelines on page 211 regarding desserts.)

Orange Pecan Streusel Muffins   **Category: B**   **Makes: 12**

Topping:
1/4 cup packed brown sugar
2 tablespoons pecan flour
1/2 teaspoon ground cinnamon
1 tablespoon melted butter

Muffins:
1 cup rice flour
1/3 cup pecan flour
1/4 cup tapioca starch
1/4 cup potato starch
1/2 cup granulated sugar
1 1/2 teaspoons Xanthan gum
2 teaspoons gluten free baking powder
1/4 teaspoon baking soda
1/2 teaspoon salt
2 tablespoons orange zest
1/2 cup chopped pecans
3/4 cup orange juice
1/4 cup vegetable oil
2 eggs

Preheat oven to 350°.

In a small bowl, combine brown sugar, pecan flour and cinnamon. Add melted butter and mix until crumbly. Set aside streusel topping.

In a large bowl, stir together rice flour, pecan flour, tapioca starch, potato starch, sugar, Xanthan gum, baking powder, baking soda, salt, orange zest and pecans. Set aside.

In a separate bowl, using an electric mixer or whisk, beat orange juice, oil and eggs until combined. Pour over dry ingredients and stir just until combined. Spoon into lightly greased muffin tin. Sprinkle streusel topping over batter. Let stand for 30 minutes.

Bake in preheated oven for 25-30 minutes or until firm to the touch. Remove from the pan immediately and let cool completely on a rack.

Serve with:
Sweet breads are best eaten alone for breakfast or as a dessert. (See guidelines on page 211 regarding desserts.)

Cornbread   **Category: B**   **Serves: 6-8**

For the oven:
1 cup rice flour
3/4 cup cornmeal
1/3 cup potato starch
1/4 cup tapioca starch
2 tablespoons granulated sugar
1 tablespoon Xanthan gum
1 tablespoon instant yeast
1 teaspoon salt
1/2 cup well drained whole kernel corn
1 cup water
1 teaspoon apple cider vinegar
1/4 cup vegetable oil
2 eggs

In a large bowl combine rice flour, cornmeal, potato starch, tapioca starch, sugar, Xanthan gum, yeast, salt, and corn. Mix well and set aside.

In a separate bowl, using a heavy duty electric mixer with paddle attachment, combine water, vinegar, oil, and eggs until well blended.

With the mixer on the lowest speed, slowly add the dry ingredients until combined. With a rubber spatula, scrape the bottom and sides of the bowl. With the mixer on medium speed, beat for 4 minutes.

Spoon the mixture into a 9 x 5 inch lightly greased pan. Let it rise, uncovered, in a warm, draft-free place for 60-75 minutes, or until the dough has risen to the top of the pan.

Meanwhile, preheat the oven to 350°. Bake for 35-45 minutes, or until a toothpick inserted in center comes out clean.

For a bread machine:
1 1/4 cups rice flour
1 cup cornmeal
1/2 cup potato starch
1/4 cup tapioca starch
3 tablespoons granulated sugar
1 tablespoon Xanthan gum
1 tablespoon instant yeast
1 1/4 teaspoon salt
1 1/4 cups water
1 teaspoon apple cider vinegar
1/4 cup vegetable oil
1/2 cup well drained whole kernel corn
4 eggs

In a large bowl combine rice flour, cornmeal, potato starch, tapioca starch, sugar, Xanthan gum, yeast, and salt. Mix well and set aside.

Pour water, vinegar, oil, and corn into bread machine baking pan. Add eggs at this time.

Select a rapid two hour basic cycle. Allow the liquids to mix until combined. Gradually add the dry ingredients as the bread machine is mixing. Scrape with a rubber spatula while adding the dry ingredients. Try to incorporate all the dry ingredients within 1-2 minutes. When the mixing and kneading are complete, leave the bread pan in the bread machine, remove the kneading blade and allow the bread machine to complete the cycle.

After baking, remove from the machine and allow the bread to remain in the pan for approximately 10 minutes. Remove the bread from the pan and cool completely before cutting.

Serve with:
Spicy Black Bean Vegetable Soup
Category A items of your choice
Category B items of your choice

Cheese Bread   **Category: B**   **Serves: 6-8**

For the oven:
1 3/4 cups white rice flour
3/4 cup brown rice flour
1/4 cup dry milk
3 tablespoons sugar
3 teaspoons Xanthan gum
2 teaspoons instant yeast
1 1/2 teaspoons salt
1 cup extra sharp Cheddar cheese, grated
1 3/4 cups water
1 teaspoon vinegar
2 tablespoons vegetable oil
3 eggs

In a large bowl or plastic bag, combine white rice flour, brown rice flour, dry milk, sugar, Xanthan gum, yeast, salt and Cheddar cheese. Mix well and set aside.

In a separate bowl, using a heavy duty electric mixer with paddle attachment, combine water, vinegar, oil and eggs until well blended.

With the mixer on the lowest speed, slowly add the dry ingredients until combined. With a rubber spatula, scrape the bottom and sides of the bowl. With the mixer on medium speed, beat for 4 minutes.

Spoon into lightly greased 9 x 5 inch pan. Let rise, uncovered, in a warm, draft-free place for 60-75 minutes or until the dough has risen to the top of the pan. Meanwhile, preheat oven to 350°. Bake for 35-45 minutes or until a toothpick inserted in center comes out clean.

For a bread machine:

2 cups white rice flour
1 cup brown rice flour
1/4 cup dry milk
3 tablespoons sugar
3 1/2 teaspoons Xanthan gum
2 1/4 teaspoons instant yeast
1 1/2 teaspoons salt
1 1/2 cups extra sharp Cheddar cheese, grated
1 1/2 cups water
1 teaspoon vinegar
3 tablespoons vegetable oil
3 eggs

In a large bowl combine white rice flour, brown rice flour, dry milk, sugar, Xanthan gum, yeast, salt and Cheddar cheese. Mix well and set aside.

Pour water, vinegar, oil, and add eggs into the bread machine baking pan.

Select a rapid two hour basic cycle. Allow the liquids to mix until combined. Gradually add the dry ingredients as the bread machine is mixing. Scrape with a rubber spatula while adding the dry ingredients. Try to incorporate all the dry ingredients within 1-2 minutes. When the mixing and kneading are completed, leave the bread pan in the bread machine, remove the kneading blade and allow the bread machine to complete the cycle.

After baking, remove from the machine and allow the bread to remain in the pan for approximately 10 minutes. Remove the bread from the pan and cool completely before cutting.

Serve with:
Chachouka
Category A items of your choice
Category B items of your choice

Rye Bread   **Category: B**   **Serves: 6-8**

For the oven:
2 cups white rice flour
1/2 cup plus 2 teaspoons brown rice flour
1/4 cup light brown sugar
1/2 cup dry milk
4 teaspoons caraway seeds
2 1/2 teaspoons Xanthan gum
2 teaspoons instant yeast
1 1/2 teaspoons salt
1 1/2 cups water
1 teaspoon vinegar
2 tablespoons molasses
1/4 cup vegetable oil
3 eggs

In a large bowl or plastic bag, combine white rice flour, brown rice flour, light brown sugar, dry milk, caraway seeds, Xanthan gum, yeast and salt. Mix well and set aside.

In a separate bowl, using a heavy duty electric mixer with paddle attachment, combine water, vinegar, molasses, oil and eggs until well blended.

With the mixer on the lowest speed, slowly add the dry ingredients until combined. With a rubber spatula, scrape the bottom and sides of the bowl. With the mixer on medium speed, beat for 4 minutes.

Spoon into lightly greased 9 x 5 inch pan. Let rise, uncovered, in a warm, draft-free place for 60-75 minutes or until the dough has risen to the top of the pan. Meanwhile, preheat oven to 350°. Bake for 35-45 minutes or until a toothpick inserted in center comes out clean.

For a bread machine:
2 1/4 cups white rice flour
3/4 cup plus 2 teaspoons brown rice flour
1/4 cup light brown sugar
1/2 cup dry milk
4 teaspoons caraway seeds
1 tablespoon Xanthan gum
2 1/4 teaspoons instant yeast
1 1/2 teaspoons salt
1 1/3 cups water
1 teaspoon vinegar
2 tablespoons molasses
1/4 cup vegetable oil
3 eggs

In a large bowl combine white rice flour, brown rice flour, light brown sugar, dry milk, caraway seeds, Xanthan gum, yeast, and salt. Mix well and set aside.

Pour water, vinegar, molasses, oil, and add eggs into the bread machine baking pan.

Select a rapid two hour basic cycle. Allow the liquids to mix until combined. Gradually add the dry ingredients as the bread machine is mixing. Scrape with a rubber spatula while adding the dry ingredients. Try to incorporate all the dry ingredients within 1-2 minutes. When the mixing and kneading are completed, leave the bread pan in the bread machine, remove the kneading blade; and allow the bread machine to complete the cycle.

After baking, remove from the machine and allow the bread to remain in the pan for approximately 10 minutes. Remove the bread from the pan and cool completely before cutting.

Serve with:
Yummy Fried Potatoes and *Sherry's Delicious Cabbage*
Category A items of your choice
Category B items of your choice

Sunflower Seed Bread   **Category: B**   **Serves: 6-8**

For the oven:
2/3 cup sorghum flour
1/2 cup amaranth flour
1/4 cup flax flour
1/2 cup potato starch
1/4 cup corn starch
3 tablespoons granulated sugar
2 1/2 teaspoons Xanthan gum
1 tablespoon instant yeast
1 1/4 teaspoons salt
1/2 cup cracked flax seed
1/2 cup raw, unsalted sunflower seeds
2 eggs
1 egg white
1 cup water
1/4 cup vegetable oil
2 teaspoons apple cider vinegar

In a large bowl combine sorghum flour, amaranth flour, flax flour, potato starch, corn starch, sugar, Xanthan gum, yeast, salt, cracked flax seed and unsalted sunflower seeds. Mix well and set aside.

In a separate bowl, using a heavy duty mixer with paddle attachment, combine eggs, egg white, water, oil, and vinegar until well blended. With the mixer on its lowest setting slowly add the dry mixture until well combined. Stop the machine and scrape the bottom and sides of the bowl with a rubber spatula. With the mixer on medium speed, beat for 4 minutes.

Spoon the mixture into a 9 x 5 inch lightly greased pan. Let it rise, uncovered, in a warm, draft-free place for 60-75 minutes, or until the dough has risen to the top of the pan.

Meanwhile, preheat the oven to 350°. Bake for 35-45 minutes, or until a toothpick inserted in center comes out clean.

For a bread machine:
3/4 cup sorghum flour
2/3 cup amaranth flour
1/3 cup flax flour
2/3 cup potato starch
1/3 cup corn starch
1/4 cup granulated sugar
2 1/2 teaspoons Xanthan gum
2 teaspoons instant yeast
1 1/2 teaspoons salt
1/2 cup cracked flax seed
1/2 cup raw, unsalted sunflower seeds
1 1/4 cups water
3 tablespoons vegetable oil
2 teaspoons apple cider vinegar
2 eggs, lightly beaten
2 egg whites, lightly beaten

In a large bowl combine sorghum flour, amaranth flour, flax flour, potato starch, corn starch, sugar, Xanthan gum, yeast, salt, flax seed, and sunflower seeds. Mix well and set aside.

Pour water, oil, and vinegar into the bread machine baking pan. Add eggs and egg whites.

Select the DOUGH cycle. As the bread machine is mixing, gradually add the dry ingredients, scraping the bottom and sides of the pan with a rubber spatula. Try to incorporate all the dry ingredients within 1-2 minutes. When the mixing and kneading are complete, remove the kneading blade, leaving the bread pan in the machine. Quickly smooth the top of the loaf; and allow the cycle to finish.

Select the BAKE cycle, and set the time to 60 minutes. The temperature should be 350°. Allow this cycle to finish. Remove the loaf from the pan immediately and let it cool on a rack.

Serve with:
Spring Greens with Beets & Goat Cheese
Category A items of your choice
Category B items of your choice

Walnut Bread   **Category: B**   **Serves: 6-8**

For the oven:
1 1/4 cups sorghum flour
1/2 cup brown rice flour
1/3 cup corn starch
1/3 cup rice bran
1 teaspoon Xanthan gum
1 tablespoon instant yeast
1 1/2 teaspoons salt
3/4 cup coarsely chopped walnuts
2 eggs
1 egg white
1 cup water
3 tablespoons walnut oil
1/3 cup honey
1 teaspoon apple cider vinegar

In a large bowl combine sorghum flour, brown rice flour, corn starch, rice bran, Xanthan gum, yeast, salt, and walnuts. Mix well and set aside.

In a separate bowl, using a heavy duty mixer with paddle attachment, combine eggs, egg white, water, walnut oil, honey, and vinegar until well blended. With the mixer on its lowest setting, slowly add the dry mixture until well combined. Stop the machine and scrape the bottom and sides of the bowl with a rubber spatula. With the mixer on medium speed, beat for 4 minutes.

Spoon the mixture into a 9 x 5 inch lightly greased pan. Let it rise, uncovered, in a warm, draft-free place for 60-75 minutes, or until the dough has risen to the top of the pan.

Meanwhile, preheat the oven to 350°. Bake for 35-45 minutes, or until a toothpick inserted in center comes out clean.

For a bread machine:
1 1/2 cups sorghum flour
3/4 cup brown rice flour
1/2 cup corn starch
1/2 cup rice bran
1 teaspoon Xanthan gum
1 1/2 teaspoons instant yeast
1 1/2 teaspoons salt
1 cup coarsely chopped walnuts
1 1/4 cups water
2 tablespoons walnut oil
1/3 cup honey
1 teaspoon apple cider vinegar
2 eggs, lightly beaten
2 egg whites, lightly beaten

In a large bowl combine sorghum flour, brown rice flour, corn starch, rice bran, Xanthan gum, yeast, salt, and walnuts. Mix well and set aside.

Pour water, walnut oil, honey, and vinegar into the bread machine baking pan. Add eggs and egg whites.

Select the DOUGH cycle. As the bread machine is mixing, gradually add the dry ingredients, scraping the bottom and sides of the pan with a rubber spatula. Try to incorporate all the dry ingredients within 1-2 minutes. When the mixing and kneading are complete, remove the kneading blade, leaving the bread pan in the machine. Quickly smooth the top of the loaf; and allow the cycle to finish.

Select the BAKE cycle, and set the time to 60 minutes. The temperature should be 350°. Allow this cycle to finish. Remove the loaf from the pan immediately and let it cool on a rack.

Serve with:
Category A items of your choice
Category B items of your choice

Herbed Italian Bread 　　　　　　　　**Category: B** 　　　　　　　　**Serves: 6-8**

For the oven:
1 1/4 cups amaranth flour
1/2 cup whole bean flour
1/3 cup potato starch
1/3 tapioca starch
1/4 cup granulated sugar
2 1/2 teaspoons Xanthan gum
2 teaspoons instant yeast
1 1/4 teaspoons salt
1/4 cup snipped fresh parsley
2 teaspoons ground, dried marjoram
2 teaspoons ground, dried thyme
2 eggs
1 1/4 cups water
1/4 cup vegetable oil
1 teaspoon apple cider vinegar

In a large bowl combine amaranth flour, whole bean flour, potato starch, tapioca starch, sugar, Xanthan gum, yeast, salt, parsley, marjoram, and thyme. Mix well and set aside.

In a separate bowl, using a heavy duty mixer with paddle attachment, combine eggs, water, oil, and vinegar until well blended. With the mixer on its lowest speed, slowly add the dry ingredients until combined. Stop the machine and scrape the bottom and sides of the bowl with a rubber spatula. With the mixer on medium speed, beat for 4 minutes.

Spoon the mixture into a 9 x 5 inch lightly greased pan. Let it rise, uncovered, in a warm, draft-free place for 60-75 minutes, or until the dough has risen to the top of the pan.

Meanwhile, preheat the oven to 350°. Bake for 35-45 minutes, or until a toothpick inserted in center comes out clean.

For a bread machine:
1 1/2 cups amaranth flour
3/4 cup whole bean flour
1/2 cup potato starch
1/4 cup tapioca starch
1/3 cup granulated sugar
1 tablespoon Xanthan gum
2 teaspoons instant yeast
1 1/2 teaspoons salt
1/4 cup snipped fresh parsley
1 tablespoon ground, dried marjoram
1 tablespoon ground, dried thyme
1 1/4 cups warm water
1/3 cup vegetable oil
1 teaspoon apple cider vinegar
2 eggs

In a large bowl combine amaranth flour, whole bean flour, potato starch, tapioca starch, sugar, Xanthan gum, yeast, salt, parsley, marjoram, and thyme. Mix well and set aside.

Pour water, oil, and vinegar into the bread machine baking pan. Add eggs.

Select the rapid two hour basic cycle. Allow the liquids to mix, gradually adding the dry mixture, scraping the bottom and sides of the pan with a rubber spatula. Try to incorporate all ingredients within 1-2 minutes.

When the mixing and kneading are complete, remove the kneading blade, leaving the bread pan in the machine. Quickly smooth the top of the loaf; and allow the cycle to finish. Remove the loaf from the pan immediately and let it cool completely on a rack.

Serve with:
Pasta Primavera
Category A items of your choice
Category B items of your choice

Cheesy Onion Bread   **Category: B**   **Serves: 6-8**

For the oven:
1 1/2 cups rice flour
1/2 cup sorghum flour
1/3 cup arrowroot starch
1/4 cup dry milk
2 tablespoons granulated sugar
2 1/2 teaspoons Xanthan gum
2 teaspoons instant yeast
1 1/4 teaspoons salt
3/4 cup shredded sharp Cheddar cheese
2 tablespoons dried onion flakes
1/4 teaspoon dry mustard
1 1/4 cups water
2 teaspoons apple cider vinegar
2 eggs
2 egg whites

In a large bowl combine rice flour, sorghum flour, arrowroot starch, dry milk, sugar, Xanthan gum, yeast, salt, cheese, onion flakes, and mustard. Mix well and set aside.

In a separate bowl, using a heavy duty mixer with paddle attachment, combine eggs, egg whites, water, and vinegar until well blended. With the mixer on its lowest speed, slowly add the dry ingredients until combined. Stop the machine and scrape the bottom and sides of the bowl with a rubber spatula. With the mixer on medium speed, beat for 4 minutes.

Spoon the mixture into a 9 x 5 inch lightly greased pan. Let it rise, uncovered, in a warm, draft-free place for 60-75 minutes, or until the dough has risen to the top of the pan.

Meanwhile, preheat the oven to 350°. Bake for 35-45 minutes, or until a toothpick inserted in center comes out clean.

For a bread machine:
1 2/3 cups rice flour
2/3 cup sorghum flour
1/3 cup arrowroot starch
1/4 cup dry milk
2 tablespoons granulated sugar
1 tablespoon Xanthan gum
1 tablespoon instant yeast
1 1/4 teaspoons salt
1 cup shredded sharp Cheddar cheese
2 tablespoons dried onion flakes
1/4 teaspoon dry mustard
1 cup water
2 teaspoons apple cider vinegar
2 eggs
2 egg whites

In a large bowl combine rice flour, sorghum flour, arrowroot starch, dry milk, sugar, Xanthan gum, yeast, salt, cheese, onion flakes, and mustard. Mix well and set aside.

Pour water and vinegar into bread machine baking pan, and add both eggs and egg whites.

Select the rapid two hour basic cycle. Allow all the liquids to mix until combined and gradually start adding the dry mixture, scraping the bottom and sides of the pan with a rubber spatula. Try to incorporate all ingredients within 1-2 minutes.

When the mixing and kneading are complete, remove the kneading blade, leaving the bread pan in the machine. Quickly smooth the top of the loaf; and allow the cycle to finish. Remove the loaf from the pan immediately and let it cool completely on a rack.

Serve with:
Potato Leek Soup
Category A items of your choice
Category B items of your choice

Nutmeg Bread   Category: B   Serves: 6-8

For the oven:
1 1/4 cups brown rice flour
1/3 cup arrowroot starch
1/3 cup quinoa flour
1/4 cup tapioca starch
2 tablespoons granulated sugar
1 tablespoon Xanthan gum
1 tablespoon instant yeast
1 1/4 teaspoons salt
1 1/4 teaspoons ground nutmeg
2/3 cup water
2/3 cup plain yogurt
1/4 cup vegetable oil
2 eggs

In a large bowl combine rice flour, arrowroot starch, quinoa flour, tapioca starch, sugar, Xanthan gum, yeast, salt, and nutmeg. Mix well and set aside.

In a separate bowl using a heavy duty mixer with paddle attachment combine water, yogurt, oil, and eggs until well blended.

With the mixer on the lowest speed, slowly add the dry ingredients until combined. With a rubber spatula, scrape the bottom and sides of the bowl. With the mixer on medium speed, beat for 4 minutes.

Spoon the mixture into a 9 x 5 inch lightly greased pan. Let it rise, uncovered, in a warm, draft-free place for 60-75 minutes, or until the dough has risen to the top of the pan.

Meanwhile, preheat the oven to 350°. Bake for 35-45 minutes, or until a toothpick inserted in center comes out clean.

For a bread machine:
1 1/4 cups brown rice flour
1/2 cup arrowroot starch
1/4 cup quinoa flour
1/4 cup tapioca starch
1/3 cup granulated sugar
1 tablespoon Xanthan gum
1 tablespoon instant yeast
1 1/4 teaspoons salt
1 1/2 teaspoons ground nutmeg
1/3 cup water
1/2 cup plain yogurt
1/4 cup vegetable oil
2 eggs

In a large bowl combine rice flour, arrowroot starch, quinoa flour, tapioca starch, sugar, Xanthan gum, yeast, salt, and nutmeg. Mix well and set aside.

Pour water, yogurt and oil into bread machine baking pan, and add eggs.

Select the rapid two hour basic cycle. Allow all the liquids to mix until combined and gradually start adding the dry mixture, scraping the bottom and sides of the pan with a rubber spatula. Try to incorporate all ingredients within 1-2 minutes.

When the mixing and kneading are complete, remove the kneading blade, leaving the bread pan in the machine. Quickly smooth the top of the loaf; and allow the cycle to finish. Remove the loaf from the pan immediately and let it cool completely on a rack.

Serve with:
Category A items of your choice
Category B items of your choice

Brown Bread   **Category: B**   **Serves: 6-8**

For the oven:
1 1/4 cups brown rice flour
1/2 cup sorghum flour
1/2 cup corn starch
1/2 cup rice bran
1 tablespoon Xanthan gum
1 tablespoon instant yeast
1 1/4 teaspoons salt
1 cup water
1 teaspoon apple cider vinegar
2 tablespoons vegetable oil
2 tablespoons liquid honey
2 tablespoons fancy molasses
3 eggs

In a large bowl combine brown rice flour, sorghum flour, corn starch, rice bran, Xanthan gum, yeast, and salt. Mix well and set aside.

In a separate bowl, using a heavy duty mixer with a paddle attachment, combine water, vinegar, oil, honey, molasses, and eggs until well blended.

With the mixer on the lowest speed, slowly add the dry ingredients to the honey mixture until it is combined. With a rubber spatula, scrape the bottom and sides of the bowl. With the mixer on medium speed, beat for 4 minutes.

Spoon the mixture into a 9 x 5 inch lightly greased pan. Let it rise, uncovered, in a warm, draft-free place for 60-75 minutes, or until the dough has risen to the top of the pan.

Meanwhile, preheat the oven to 350°. Bake for 35-45 minutes, or until a toothpick inserted in center comes out clean.

For a bread machine:
1 1/2 cups brown rice flour
1/2 cup sorghum flour
1/2 cup corn starch
1/2 cup rice bran
1 tablespoon Xanthan gum
1 tablespoon instant yeast
1 1/4 teaspoons salt
1 cup water
1 teaspoon apple cider vinegar
2 tablespoons vegetable oil
2 tablespoons liquid honey
2 tablespoons fancy molasses
3 eggs

In a large bowl combine brown rice flour, sorghum flour, corn starch, rice bran, Xanthan gum, yeast, and salt. Mix well and set aside.

Pour water, vinegar, oil, honey, and molasses into the bread machine baking pan, and add the eggs.

Select the rapid two hour basic cycle. Allow all the liquids to mix until combined and gradually start adding the dry mixture, scraping the bottom and sides of the pan with a rubber spatula. Try to incorporate all ingredients within 1-2 minutes.

When the mixing and kneading are complete, remove the kneading blade, leaving the bread pan in the machine. Quickly smooth the top of the loaf; and allow the cycle to finish. Remove the loaf from the pan immediately and let it cool completely on a rack.

Serve with:
Yellow Tomato Soup with Goat Cheese Croutons
Category A items of your choice
Category B items of your choice

Buckwheat Nut Bread   **Category: B**   **Serves: 6-8**

For the oven:
1 cup whole bean flour
1/3 cup buckwheat flour
1/2 cup potato starch
1/4 cup tapioca starch
1/4 cup packed brown sugar
2 teaspoons Xanthan gum
1 tablespoon instant yeast
1 teaspoon salt
3/4 teaspoon ground cardamom
3/4 cup chopped walnuts
1 1/4 cups water
1 teaspoon apple cider vinegar
3 tablespoons vegetable oil
2 eggs

In a large bowl combine whole bean flour, buckwheat flour, potato starch, tapioca starch, brown sugar, Xanthan gum, yeast, salt, cardamom, and walnuts. Mix well and set aside.

In a separate bowl using a heavy duty mixer with paddle attachment, combine water, vinegar, oil, and eggs until well blended. With the mixer on the lowest speed slowly add the dry ingredients to the mixture. With a rubber spatula, scrape the bottom and sides of the bowl. With the mixer now on medium speed, beat for 4 minutes.

Spoon the mixture into a lightly greased 9 x 5 inch pan. Allow it to rise, uncovered, in a warm draft-free place for 60-75 minutes, or until the dough has risen to the top of the pan. Meanwhile preheat the oven to 350°. Bake for 35-45 minutes or until a toothpick inserted in center comes out clean.

For a bread machine:
1 1/4 cups whole bean flour
1/2 cup buckwheat flour
1/2 cup potato starch
1/4 cup tapioca starch
1/3 cup packed brown sugar
1 tablespoon Xanthan gum
1 tablespoon instant yeast
1 1/4 teaspoon salt
1 teaspoon ground cardamom
1 cup chopped walnuts
1 1/3 cups water
1 teaspoon apple cider vinegar
1/4 cup vegetable oil
2 eggs

In a large bowl combine whole bean flour, buckwheat flour, potato starch, tapioca starch, brown sugar, Xanthan gum, yeast, salt, cardamom, and walnuts. Mix well and set aside.

Pour water, vinegar, and oil into the bread machine pan and add the eggs.

Select the rapid two hour basic cycle. Allow the liquids to mix until combined. Gradually add the dry ingredients as the bread machine is mixing. Scrape with a rubber spatula while adding the dry ingredients. Try to incorporate all the dry ingredients within 1-2 minutes. When the mixing and kneading are complete, remove the kneading blade, leaving the bread pan in the machine. Allow the bread machine to complete the cycle.

After baking, remove from the machine and allow the bread to remain in the pan for approximately 10 minutes. Remove the bread from the pan and cool completely before cutting.

Serve with:
Category A items of your choice
Category B items of your choice

Pumpernickel Bread   **Category: B**   **Serves: 6-8**

For the oven:
3/4 cup whole bean flour
3/4 cup yellow pea flour
1/2 cup potato starch
1/4 cup tapioca starch
2 tablespoons packed brown sugar
2 teaspoons Xanthan gum
1 tablespoon instant yeast
1 1/4 teaspoons salt
2 teaspoons instant coffee grounds
2 teaspoons unsweetened cocoa powder
1/2 teaspoon ground ginger
1 1/4 cups water
2 tablespoons fancy molasses
1 teaspoon apple cider vinegar
2 tablespoons vegetable oil
2 eggs

In a large bowl combine whole bean flour, yellow pea flour, potato starch, tapioca starch, brown sugar, Xanthan gum, yeast, salt, coffee, cocoa, and ginger. Mix well and set aside.

In a separate bowl, using a heavy duty mixer with paddle attachment, combine water, molasses, vinegar, oil, and eggs until well blended. With the mixer on the lowest speed slowly add the dry ingredients to the mixture. With a rubber spatula, scrape the bottom and sides of the bowl. With the mixer now on medium speed, beat for 4 minutes.

Spoon the mixture into a lightly greased 9 x 5 inch pan. Allow it to rise, uncovered, in a warm draft-free place for 60-75 minutes, or until the dough has risen to the top of the pan. Meanwhile preheat the oven to 350°. Bake for 35-45 minutes or until a toothpick inserted in center comes out clean.

For a bread machine:
1 cup whole bean flour
1 cup yellow pea flour
2/3 cup potato starch
1/3 cup tapioca starch
3 tablespoons packed brown sugar
2 1/2 teaspoons Xanthan gum
1 tablespoon instant yeast
1 1/2 teaspoons salt
1 tablespoon instant coffee granules
1 tablespoon unsweetened cocoa powder
1/2 teaspoon ground ginger
1 1/2 cups water
3 tablespoons fancy molasses
1 teaspoon apple cider vinegar
2 tablespoons vegetable oil
3 eggs

In a large bowl, combine whole bean flour, yellow pea flour, potato starch, tapioca starch, brown sugar, Xanthan gum, yeast, salt, coffee, cocoa, and ginger. Mix well and set aside.

Pour water, molasses, vinegar, and oil into the bread machine pan. Add the eggs.

Select the rapid two hour basic cycle. Allow the liquids to mix until combined. Gradually add the dry ingredients as the bread machine is mixing. Scrape with a rubber spatula while adding the dry ingredients. Try to incorporate all the dry ingredients within 1-2 minutes. When the mixing and kneading are complete, remove the kneading blade, leaving the bread pan in the machine. Allow the bread machine to complete the cycle.

After baking, remove from the machine and allow the bread to remain in the pan for approximately 10 minutes. Remove the bread from the pan and cool completely before cutting.

Serve with:

French Onion Soup
Category A items of your choice
Category B items of your choice

Multi-Grain Bread   **Category: B**   **Serves: 6-8**

For the oven:
1 cup sorghum flour
2/3 cup amaranth flour
1/2 cup cornmeal
1/4 cup quinoa flour
1/3 cup tapioca starch
1/3 cup packed brown sugar
1 tablespoon Xanthan gum
1 tablespoon instant yeast
1 1/2 teaspoons salt
2 eggs
1 egg white
1 cup water
2 tablespoons vegetable oil
1 teaspoon apple cider vinegar

In a large bowl combine sorghum flour, amaranth flour, cornmeal, quinoa flour, tapioca starch, brown sugar, Xanthan gum, yeast, and salt. Mix well and set aside.

In a separate bowl, using a heavy duty mixer with paddle attachment, combine eggs, egg white, water, oil, and vinegar until well blended. With the mixer on the lowest speed slowly add the dry ingredients to the mixture. With a rubber spatula, scrape the bottom and sides of the bowl. With the mixer now on medium speed, beat for 4 minutes.

Spoon the mixture into a lightly greased 9 x 5 inch pan. Allow it to rise, uncovered in a warm draft-free place for 60-75 minutes, or until the dough has risen to the top of the pan. Meanwhile preheat the oven to 350°. Bake for 35-45 minutes or until a toothpick inserted in center comes out clean.

For a bread machine:
1 cup sorghum flour
3/4 cup amaranth flour
3/4 cup cornmeal
1/4 cup quinoa flour
1/2 cup tapioca starch
1/3 cup packed brown sugar
1 tablespoon Xanthan gum
3/4 teaspoon instant yeast
1 1/2 teaspoons salt
1 1/4 cups water
2 tablespoons vegetable oil
1 teaspoon apple cider vinegar
2 eggs, lightly beaten
2 egg whites, lightly beaten

In a large bowl combine sorghum flour, amaranth flour, cornmeal, quinoa flour, tapioca starch, brown sugar, Xanthan gum, yeast, and salt. Mix well and set aside.

Pour water, oil, and vinegar into the bread machine pan. Add the eggs and egg whites.

Select the DOUGH cycle. As the bread machine is mixing, gradually add the dry ingredients, scraping the bottom and sides of the pan with a rubber spatula. Try to incorporate all the dry ingredients within 1-2 minutes. When the mixing and kneading are complete, remove the kneading blade, leaving the bread pan in the machine. Quickly smooth the top of the loaf; and allow the cycle to finish.

Select the BAKE cycle, and set the time to 60 minutes. The temperature should be 350°. Allow this cycle to finish. Remove the loaf from the pan immediately and let it cool on a rack.

Serve with:
Arugula Salad with Garlic Balsamic Vinaigrette
Category A items of your choice
Category B items of your choice

Roasted Garlic Bread **Category: B** **Serves: 6-8**

For the oven:
1 cup brown rice flour
3/4 cup almond flour
1/2 cup amaranth flour
1/4 cup potato starch
1 tablespoon Xanthan gum
1 tablespoon instant yeast
1 1/2 teaspoons salt
1/4 cup mashed potatoes
2 eggs
1 egg white
1 1/4 cups water
2 tablespoons extra virgin olive oil
3 cloves roasted garlic (see instructions for roasting garlic on page 69)
2 tablespoons liquid honey
1 teaspoon apple cider vinegar

In a large bowl combine rice flour, almond flour, amaranth flour, potato starch, Xanthan gum, yeast, salt, and mashed potatoes. Mix well and set aside.

In a separate bowl, using a heavy duty mixer with paddle attachment, combine eggs, egg whites, water, olive oil, garlic, honey, and vinegar until well blended. With the mixer on the lowest speed slowly add the dry ingredients to the mixture. With a rubber spatula, scrape the bottom and sides of the bowl. With the mixer now on medium speed, beat for 4 minutes.

Spoon the mixture into a lightly greased 9 x 5 inch pan. Allow it to rise, uncovered in a warm draft-free place for 60-75 minutes, or until the dough has risen to the top of the pan. Meanwhile preheat the oven to 350°. Bake for 35-45 minutes or until a toothpick inserted in center comes out clean.

For a bread machine:
1 cup brown rice flour
1 cup almond flour
1/2 cup amaranth flour
1/3 cup potato starch
1 tablespoon Xanthan gum
1 3/4 teaspoons instant yeast
1 1/2 teaspoons salt
1/3 cup mashed potatoes
1 1/3 cups water
2 tablespoons extra virgin olive oil
3 tablespoons liquid honey
1 teaspoon apple cider vinegar
3 cloves roasted garlic (see instructions for roasting garlic on page 69)
2 eggs, lightly beaten
2 egg whites, lightly beaten

In a large bowl combine rice flour, almond flour, amaranth flour, potato starch, Xanthan gum, yeast, salt, and mashed potatoes. Mix well and set aside.

Pour water, oil, honey, vinegar, and garlic into the bread machine pan. Add eggs, and egg whites.

Select the DOUGH cycle. As the bread machine is mixing, gradually add the dry ingredients, scraping the bottom and sides of the pan with a rubber spatula. Try to incorporate all the dry ingredients within 1-2 minutes. When the mixing and kneading are complete, remove the kneading blade, leaving the bread pan in the machine. Quickly smooth the top of the loaf; and allow the cycle to finish.

Select the BAKE cycle, and set the time to 60 minutes. The temperature should be 350°. Allow this cycle to finish. Remove the loaf from the pan immediately and let it cool on a rack.

Serve with:
Spinach Stuffed Portobellos
Category A items of your choice
Category B items of your choice

Sourdough Starter to be used with Sourdough Bread Recipes

3 cups warm water
2 tablespoons granulated sugar
2 tablespoons instant yeast
3 cups sorghum flour

In a very large glass bowl, combine the water and sugar. Sprinkle with yeast, gently stir to moisten and let stand for 10 minutes.

Add sorghum flour and whisk until smooth.

Cover with a double layer of cheesecloth, or a loose fitting lid. Secure so that it is not touching the starter. Let stand at room temperature for 2-4 days stirring 2 to 3 times a day. When ready to use, starter will have a sour smell with small bubbles rising to the surface, this is normal.

Store loosely covered in the refrigerator until needed. If not used regularly, stir in 1 teaspoon of granulated sugar every 10 days.

Sourdough Bread   **Category: B**   **Serves: 6-8**

For the oven:
1 cup brown rice flour
3/4 cup amaranth flour
1/3 cup potato starch
2 tablespoons granulated sugar
1 tablespoon Xanthan gum
1 tablespoon instant yeast
1 1/2 teaspoons salt
2 egg whites
1 egg
1 cup Sourdough Starter at room temperature (See page 46)
1/4 cup water
2 tablespoons vegetable oil

In a large bowl combine rice flour, amaranth flour, potato starch, sugar, Xanthan gum, yeast, and salt. Mix well and set aside.

In a separate bowl, using a heavy duty mixer with a paddle attachment, combine eggs whites, egg, Sourdough Starter, water, and oil until well blended. With the mixer on the lowest speed slowly add the dry ingredients to the mixture. With a rubber spatula, scrape the bottom and sides of the bowl. With the mixer now on medium speed, beat for 4 minutes.

Spoon the mixture into a lightly greased 9 x 5 inch pan. Allow it to rise, uncovered in a warm draft-free place for 60-75 minutes, or until the dough has risen to the top of the pan. Meanwhile preheat the oven to 350°. Bake for 35-45 minutes or until a toothpick inserted in center comes out clean.

For a bread machine:
1 cup brown rice flour
1 cup amaranth flour
1/2 cup potato starch
2 tablespoons granulated sugar
1 tablespoon Xanthan gum
1 tablespoon instant yeast
1 1/2 teaspoons salt
1 cup Sourdough Starter at room temperature (See page 46)
1/4 cup water
1/4 cup vegetable oil
2 eggs, lightly beaten
2 egg whites, lightly beaten

In a large bowl combine rice flour, amaranth flour, potato starch, sugar, Xanthan gum, yeast, and salt. Mix well and set aside.

Pour Sourdough Starter, water, and oil into the bread machine pan. Add eggs, and egg whites.

Select the DOUGH cycle. As the bread machine is mixing, gradually add the dry ingredients, scraping the bottom and sides of the pan with a rubber spatula. Try to incorporate all the dry ingredients within 1-2 minutes. When the mixing and kneading are complete, remove the kneading blade, leaving the bread pan in the machine. Quickly smooth the top of the loaf; and allow the cycle to finish.

Select the BAKE cycle, and set the time to 60 minutes. The temperature should be 350°. Allow this cycle to finish. Remove the loaf from the pan immediately and let it cool on a rack.

Serve with:
Quinoa and Black Bean Salad
Category A items of your choice
Category B items of your choice

Sourdough Brown Bread   **Category: B**   **Serves: 6-8**

For the oven:
1 cup sorghum flour
1/2 cup whole bean flour
1/3 cup tapioca starch
1 tablespoon Xanthan gum
1 tablespoon instant yeast
1 1/4 teaspoons salt
2 eggs
1 cup Sourdough Starter at room temperature (See page 46)
1/2 cup water
2 tablespoons vegetable oil
2 tablespoons liquid honey
1 tablespoon molasses

In a large bowl combine sorghum flour, whole bean flour, tapioca starch, Xanthan gum, yeast, and salt. Mix well and set aside.

In a separate bowl, using a heavy duty mixer with paddle attachment, combine eggs, Sourdough Starter, water, oil, honey, and molasses until well blended. With the mixer on the lowest speed slowly add the dry ingredients to the mixture. With a rubber spatula, scrape the bottom and sides of the bowl. With the mixer now on medium speed, beat for 4 minutes.

Spoon the mixture into a lightly greased 9 x 5 inch pan. Allow it to rise, uncovered in a warm draft-free place for 60-75 minutes, or until the dough has risen to the top of the pan. Meanwhile preheat the oven to 350°. Bake for 35-45 minutes or until the a toothpick inserted in center comes out clean.

For a bread machine:
1 cup sorghum flour
2/3 cup whole bean flour
1/3 cup tapioca starch
1 tablespoon Xanthan gum
1 tablespoon instant yeast
1 1/4 teaspoons salt
1 cup Sourdough Starter at room temperature (See page 46)
3/4 cup water
2 tablespoons vegetable oil
2 tablespoons liquid honey
2 tablespoons molasses
2 eggs, lightly beaten

In a large bowl combine sorghum flour, whole bean flour, tapioca starch, Xanthan gum, yeast, and salt. Mix well and set aside.

Pour Sourdough Starter, water, oil, honey, and molasses into the bread machine pan. Add eggs.

Select the DOUGH cycle. As the bread machine is mixing, gradually add the dry ingredients, scraping the bottom and sides of the pan with a rubber spatula. Try to incorporate all the dry ingredients within 1-2 minutes. When the mixing and kneading are complete, remove the kneading blade, leaving the bread pan in the machine. Quickly smooth the top of the loaf; and allow the cycle to finish.

Select the BAKE cycle, and set the time to 60 minutes. The temperature should be 350°. Allow this cycle to finish. Remove the loaf from the pan immediately and let it cool on a rack.

Serve with:
Roasted Winter Vegetable Soup
Category A items of your choice
Category B items of your choice

Sourdough Walnut Bread **Category: B** **Serves: 6-8**

For the oven:
1 cup amaranth flour
1/2 cup quinoa flour
1/3 cup tapioca starch
1/4 cup packed brown sugar
1 tablespoon Xanthan gum
1 1/2 teaspoons instant yeast
1 1/4 teaspoons salt
3/4 cup chopped walnuts
2 eggs
1 cup Sourdough Starter at room temperature (See page 46)
1/2 cup water
2 tablespoons vegetable oil

In a large bowl combine amaranth flour, quinoa flour, tapioca starch, brown sugar, Xanthan gum, yeast, salt, and walnuts. Mix well and set aside.

In a separate bowl, using a heavy duty mixer with paddle attachment, combine eggs, Sourdough Starter, water, and oil until well blended. With the mixer on the lowest speed slowly add the dry ingredients to the mixture. With a rubber spatula, scrape the bottom and sides of the bowl. With the mixer now on medium speed, beat for 4 minutes.

Spoon the mixture into a lightly greased 9 x 5 inch pan. Allow it to rise, uncovered in a warm draft-free place for 60-75 minutes, or until the dough has risen to the top of the pan. Meanwhile preheat the oven to 350°. Bake for 35-45 minutes or until a toothpick inserted in center comes out clean.

For a bread machine:
1 1/4 cups amaranth flour
1/2 cup quinoa flour
1/2 cup tapioca starch
1/4 cup packed brown sugar
1 tablespoon Xanthan gum
1 1/2 teaspoons instant yeast
1 1/4 teaspoons salt
1 cup chopped walnuts
1 cup Sourdough Starter at room temperature (See page 46)
2/3 cup water
2 tablespoons vegetable oil
2 eggs, lightly beaten

In a large bowl combine amaranth flour, quinoa flour, tapioca starch, brown sugar, Xanthan gum, yeast, salt, and walnuts. Mix well and set aside.

Pour Sourdough Starter, water, and oil into the bread machine pan. Add eggs.

Select the DOUGH cycle. As the bread machine is mixing, gradually add the dry ingredients, scraping the bottom and sides of the pan with a rubber spatula. Try to incorporate all the dry ingredients within 1-2 minutes. When the mixing and kneading are complete, remove the kneading blade, leaving the bread pan in the machine. Quickly smooth the top of the loaf; and allow the cycle to finish.

Select the BAKE cycle, and set the time to 60 minutes. The temperature should be 350°. Allow this cycle to finish. Remove the loaf from the pan immediately and let it cool on a rack.

Serve with:
Tossed Salad
Category A items of your choice
Category B items of your choice

Tomato Rosemary Bread   **Category: B**   **Serves: 6-8**

For the oven:
1 cup sorghum flour
1/2 cup whole bean flour
1/3 cup corn starch
3 tablespoons granulated sugar
1 tablespoon Xanthan gum
1 tablespoon instant yeast
1/2 teaspoon salt
1 1/2 teaspoons crushed rosemary
1/3 cup chopped sun-dried tomatoes
1 1/4 cups tomato juice, room temperature
1/4 cup vegetable oil
2 eggs

In a large bowl combine sorghum flour, whole bean flour, corn starch, sugar, Xanthan gum, yeast, salt, rosemary, and tomatoes. Mix well and set aside.

In a separate bowl, using a heavy duty mixer with paddle attachment, combine juice, oil, and eggs until well blended. With the mixer on the lowest speed, slowly add the dry ingredients until combined. With a rubber spatula, scrape the bottom and sides of the bowl. With the mixer on medium speed, beat for 4 minutes.

Spoon the mixture into a lightly greased 9 x 5 inch loaf pan. Let it rise uncovered, in a warm draft-free place for 60–75 minutes or until the dough has risen to the top of the pan. Meanwhile, preheat the oven to 350°. Bake for 34–45 minutes or until a toothpick inserted in center comes out clean.

For a bread machine:
1 cup sorghum flour
1/2 cup whole bean flour
1/2 cup corn starch
1/4 cup granulated sugar
1 tablespoon Xanthan gum
1 tablespoon instant yeast
1/2 teaspoon salt
2 teaspoons crushed rosemary
1/2 cup chopped sun-dried tomatoes
1 1/4 cups tomato juice, room temperature
1/4 cup vegetable oil
2 eggs

In a large bowl combine sorghum flour, whole bean flour, corn starch, sugar, Xanthan gum, yeast, salt, rosemary, and tomatoes. Mix well and set aside.

Pour juice and oil into the bread machine baking pan. Add eggs.

Select the rapid two hour basic cycle. Allow the liquids to mix until combined. Gradually add the dry ingredients as the bread machine is mixing. Scrape with a rubber spatula while adding the dry ingredients. Try to incorporate all the dry ingredients within 1-2 minutes. When the mixing and kneading are complete, remove the kneading blade, leaving the bread pan in the machine. Allow the bread machine to complete the cycle.

After baking, remove from the machine and allow the bread to remain in the pan for approximately 10 minutes. Remove the bread from the pan and cool completely before cutting.

Serve with:
White Bean Stew with Swiss Chard and Tomatoes
Category A items of your choice
Category B items of your choice

Gingerbread   **Category: B**   **Serves: 6-8**

1 cup boiling water
1/2 cup shortening
3/4 cup whole bean flour
3/4 cup sorghum flour
1/4 cup tapioca starch
1 teaspoon Xanthan gum
1/2 teaspoon gluten free baking powder
1/4 teaspoon baking soda
1/4 teaspoon salt
1 1/2 teaspoon ground ginger
3/4 teaspoon ground cinnamon
2 eggs
2/3 cup fancy molasses
2/3 cup granulated sugar

Preheat oven to 350°. Lightly grease an 8 inch square baking pan

In a small bowl, pour boiling water over shortening. Set aside to melt and cool slightly.

In a large bowl, sift together whole bean flour, sorghum flour, tapioca starch, Xanthan gum, baking powder, baking soda, salt, ginger and cinnamon. Resift and set aside.

In a separate bowl, using an electric mixer, beat eggs, molasses and sugar. Add shortening mixture and beat until smooth. Stir in dry ingredients. Mix until blended. Pour into prepared pan. Let stand for 30 minutes before baking.

Bake in preheated oven for 45-55 minutes or until a toothpick inserted in the center comes out clean. Let cool in the pan on a rack for 10 minutes. Remove from pan and serve warm.

<u>Serve with:</u>
Sweet breads are best eaten alone for breakfast or as a dessert. (See guidelines on page 211 regarding desserts.)

Condiments

Condiments have not been assigned a food category since they are used in such small amounts and usually do not affect digestion of other foods.

Apple Butter   **Makes: 5-6 cups**

9-10 Macintosh apples, peeled and cored
1 cup apple cider
2 teaspoons apple pie spice (or 1/2 teaspoon each of nutmeg and allspice and 1 teaspoon cinnamon)

Cut the apples into 1 inch chunks (don't worry about making them perfectly sized). Place them in a large sauce pan and pour apple cider over them. Add apple pie spice. Cover and cook for about 30 minutes over low heat until the apples are soft.

Cool the apple mixture, divide it into two batches and purée each in a food processor or blender. At this point you will have unsweetened apple sauce.

Pour the pureed fruit into a 13 x 9 x 2 inch pan and then spread mixture evenly.

Bake in a 300° oven for 2-3 hours, until thick and deep brown; stirring every 20 minutes.

Cool the apple butter and then scoop it into a clean jar with a sealable lid. This will keep in the refrigerator for 2 months.

Serve with:
Use as a topping for ice cream, *Pancakes, Waffles* or *Cornbread*

The Best Thousand Island Dressing   **Makes: 3 cups**

2 cups mayonnaise
1 hard-boiled egg, finely chopped
2 tablespoons gluten free Worcestershire sauce
1 1/2 teaspoons sugar
2 tablespoons apple cider vinegar
6 tablespoons sweet pickle relish
1/4 cup chopped black olives
1/2 cup diced red bell pepper

Combine all ingredients and chill.

Serve over mixed salad greens or as a dressing for sandwiches.

Spicy French Dressing   **Makes: 2 3/4 cups**

1 cup ketchup
3/4 cup olive oil
1/2 cup maple syrup
1/2 cup apple cider vinegar
1/2 teaspoon dry mustard
1/2 teaspoon ground ginger
1/2 teaspoon salt
1/2 teaspoon pepper
1 garlic clove, crushed

Whisk all ingredients together or blend in a blender on high speed for 30 seconds.

Coci Helen's Salad Dressing   **Makes: 3 1/2 cups**

2 cups mayonnaise
1 1/2 cups buttermilk
2 tablespoons white wine vinegar
1/2 cup chopped fresh chives
1/2 teaspoon sugar
Salt and pepper to taste

Whisk all ingredients together until smooth and well-combined. Chill.

Spoon over mixed green salad or use as a dip for vegetables.

Fresh Salsa   **Makes: 2 1/2 cups**

2 lbs. ripe tomatoes (about 5 medium)
1–2 fresh jalapeno peppers (depending on your desired amount of "heat")
1/4 cup finely chopped white onion
1/2 cup fresh cilantro sprigs, chopped
3 cloves garlic, minced
1 teaspoon sugar
1 1/2 tablespoons fresh lime juice
Salt and pepper to taste

Seed tomatoes, dice into 1/4 inch pieces and place in bowl.

Seed and finely chop jalapenos, being careful not to touch your hands to your eyes. Add jalapenos to bowl and wash hands thoroughly with soap and water.

Add remaining ingredients to bowl; stir to combine.

This keeps for about 1 week in the refrigerator.

<u>Serve with:</u>
Tortilla chips
Cornbread
Your favorite Mexican dishes

Mango Salsa   **Makes: 2 cups**

3 mangos, chopped
5–7 chili peppers, seeded and chopped
1 small onion, minced
1/4 cup cilantro or fresh parsley
1/2 teaspoon salt
Juice from 2 limes

Mix all ingredients in a bowl, food processor or blender. Refrigerate 1-2 hours before serving.

Serve with:
Broiled fish
Gluten free tortilla chips

Parsley Pesto   **Makes: 1/2 cup**

1 1/2 cups chopped fresh parsley
2 large cloves garlic, quartered
3 tablespoons Parmesan cheese
1 tablespoon white wine vinegar
1/4 cup olive oil
Salt and pepper to taste

Combine parsley, garlic, cheese and vinegar in a food processor. Process until finely chopped.

Keeping the motor running, pour oil through the food tube in a slow, steady stream.

Add salt and pepper and process just to combine.

This is a great addition to soups, stews, and pasta, or mix a spoonful with olive oil and use as a bread dip.

Basil Pesto   **Makes: 2/3 cup**

40 fresh basil leaves
2 tablespoons pine nuts
2 large cloves garlic, chopped
1/4 cup Parmesan cheese
2 tablespoons Romano cheese
7 tablespoons olive oil
2 tablespoons hot water or Vegetable broth
Salt and pepper to taste

Combine basil, pine nuts, garlic, cheeses and half of the oil in a food processor. Process until finely chopped.

Keeping the motor running, pour broth, remaining oil, salt and pepper through the food tube.

This is a great addition to soups, stews, and pasta, or mix a spoonful with olive oil and use as a bread dip.

Easy Homemade Pickles   **Makes: 3 quarts**

10 unpeeled large cucumbers, very thinly sliced
3 cups water
3 cups white vinegar
2 1/2 cups sugar
1/4 cup salt
1/4 cup chopped fresh parsley
1 tablespoon celery seed
Pinch of white pepper
1 large onion, thinly sliced

In a large mixing bowl, combine water, vinegar, sugar, salt, parsley, celery seeds and pepper.

Add cucumbers and onions, mix well to combine.

Divide into clean jars and cover tightly. Refrigerate at least 6 hours before serving.

Italian Butter (Bread Dipping Oil)   **Makes: 1 cup**

1 cup olive oil
1 tablespoon grated Parmesan or Romano cheese
1 tablespoon chopped fresh parsley
1 tablespoon chopped basil leaves
1 teaspoon dried oregano
2-3 cloves garlic, pressed
1/2 teaspoon salt
1 teaspoon freshly ground black pepper

Combine all ingredients. Serve in shallow bowls or small plates with gluten-free bread slices.

Roasted Garlic Spread   **Makes: 1 1/4 cups**

1 large head garlic, unpeeled
1 tablespoon olive oil
1-8 oz. package cream cheese, softened
1/4 cup butter or margarine, softened
1/2 teaspoon salt
2 tablespoons minced fresh chives

Instructions for roasting garlic:
Peel outer skin from garlic. Place garlic in a small baking pan; drizzle with oil. Cover with aluminum foil. Bake at 350° for 25 minutes. Remove cover, and bake 8-10 additional minutes or until garlic is soft. Remove from oven, and let cool completely. Remove and discard papery skin from garlic. Scoop out garlic pulp with a small spoon.

Beat cream cheese and butter at high speed with an electric mixer until light and fluffy. Add garlic and salt; beat until blended. Stir in chives. Store spread in refrigerator. Serve over warm slices of gluten free French bread or on gluten free crackers.

Teriyaki Marinade   **Makes: 1 1/4 cups**

1/2 cup gluten free tamari (soy sauce)
1/4 cup brown sugar
1/2 cup orange juice
2 cloves garlic, minced
1/2 teaspoon black pepper

Combine all ingredients in a small (non-metal) bowl. Pour over beef, fish or chicken and marinate for at least 3 hours.

Honey Mustard Vinaigrette   **Makes: 2 cups**

1/3 cup apple cider vinegar
1/3 cup Dijon mustard
1/3 cup honey
1 cup canola oil
Salt to taste

Whisk together all ingredients. Add salt to taste.

Cover and store in refrigerator.

Serve over mixed green or use as a basting sauce for grilling or broiling chicken or fish.

Salads

Antipasto   **Category: A/C**   **Serves: 4-6**

1 large or 2 small heads romaine lettuce, rinsed, dried and chopped

Choose desired toppings below:
3/4 lb. Italian cheese, sliced, such as fresh Mozzarella, Provolone, Asiago, or Parmigiano-Reggiano
1/4 lb. salami, sliced
1/4 lb. prosciutto, sliced
1-7 1/2 oz. jar roasted red peppers, drained
1-14 1/2 oz. can artichoke hearts, drained and sliced
4 hard boiled eggs, sliced
2/3 cup jarred hot cherry peppers or pickled pepperoncini, drained
1 cup gluten free Kalamata or black olives
Vinaigrette, balsamic vinaigrette, or gluten free Caesar dressing

Cover a large serving tray or platter with a bed of lettuce. Drizzle with gluten free salad dressing of choice. Arrange remaining ingredients neatly on top of the bed of lettuce.

Serve with:
If you are not having meat on your salad, you may serve with *Herbed Italian Bread* or other gluten free bread of your choice.
If you are having meat on your salad, you may serve with Category A items of your choice and Category C items of your choice.

Calamari Salad   Category: C   Serves: 6-8

2 1/2 lbs. frozen calamari, body and tentacles, thawed (frozen calamari is typically sold in 2 1/2 lb. packages)
1/4 lemon
3 celery stalks, sliced
1 cup red bell pepper, diced
1/2 red onion, diced
1/2 cup large capers, drained
12-15 gluten free Kalamata olives, pitted and halved
12-15 gluten free Spanish pimento-stuffed olives
8 pepperoncini, stemmed and sliced into rings
1 cup fresh basil, chopped
1/2 cup olive oil
1/2 cup white Balsamic vinegar or other white vinegar
1 1/2 teaspoons garlic powder
1 teaspoon salt
1 1/2 teaspoons ground black pepper

Chop calamari bodies into 1/2 inch pieces, but do not cut tentacles. In a large pot, bring 8 cups of water to a boil. Add salt and lemon to the water. Add the calamari and boil for 1 hour uncovered. Drain, but do not rinse.

Transfer calamari to a bowl, add remaining ingredients and toss well. Cover tightly with plastic wrap and marinate over night in the refrigerator.

To serve, line a shallow bowl with lettuce and spoon calamari mixture over the lettuce.

Serve with:
Category A items of your choice
Category C items of your choice

Cobb Salad   **Category: A/C**   **Serves: 6-8**

Vinaigrette:
1 teaspoon Dijon mustard
1 medium garlic clove, minced or pressed
1/4 teaspoon sugar
1/2 teaspoon salt
1/8 teaspoon ground black pepper
1 teaspoon Worcestershire sauce
2 teaspoons fresh lemon juice
2 tablespoons red wine vinegar
1/2 cup extra virgin olive oil

Salad:
6 boneless, skinless chicken breast halves, trimmed of excess fat
1 large head romaine lettuce, washed, dried and torn into bite size pieces
1 bunch arugula, washed and dried, with stems removed
1 pint cherry tomatoes, halved
3 hardboiled eggs, sliced
2 medium ripe avocados, pitted and sliced
2 oz. Blue cheese crumbles
3 tablespoons minced fresh chives
Salt, ground black pepper and garlic powder

For the vinaigrette: Whisk all the ingredients together in a medium bowl until well combined; set aside.

For the salad: Season the chicken with salt, pepper and garlic powder. Adjust an oven rack to 6 inches from the broiler element; heat the broiler. Spray the broiler pan top with cooking spray and place the chicken breasts on top and broil until golden brown; 4-8 minutes. Using tongs, flip the chicken and continue to broil until cooked; about another 6-8 minutes. When cool enough to handle, cut chicken into 1/4 inch slices and set aside.

Toss the romaine and arugula with 5 tablespoons of the vinaigrette in a large bowl until coated; arrange on a large flat platter. Place the chicken in a bowl and add 1/2 cup of the vinaigrette, toss to coat. Arrange the chicken in a row along one edge of the greens. Place the tomatoes in the bowl and add 1 tablespoon of the vinaigrette, toss to coat and arrange on the opposite edge of greens. Arrange the eggs and avocados near the center and drizzle the remaining vinaigrette. Sprinkle the cheese and chives evenly over the salad and serve.

Serve with:
Category A items of your choice
Category C items of your choice

Caprese Salad   **Category: A/C**   **Serves: 6-8**

3 large vine ripened tomatoes
1/2 lb. fresh Mozzarella cheese, the freshest and best quality you can find
12 fresh basil leaves
1/4 cup extra virgin olive oil
2 tablespoons Balsamic vinegar
1 1/2 teaspoons garlic powder
Salt and fresh ground pepper to taste

Halve the tomatoes then cut into thin slices 1/4 inch thick. Slice the Mozzarella into 1/2 inch thick rounds. Cut the basil leaves into thin strips.

On a serving platter, alternate tomato and Mozzarella slices, overlapping slightly. Drizzle with the olive oil and Balsamic vinegar, and then sprinkle with the shredded basil. Season with garlic powder, salt, and pepper.

Serve with:
Category A items of your choice
Category C items of your choice

Spinach Salad with Beets & Feta Cheese   Category: A   **Serves: 4-6**

1/2 cup pine nuts
2 tablespoons balsamic vinegar
1/4 cup extra virgin olive oil
2 tablespoons maple syrup
1 teaspoon whole grain or Dijon mustard
1/8 teaspoon salt
1 lb. fresh baby spinach
1 lb. fresh beets, or 1-14 1/2 oz. can sliced beets, drained
1 cup crumbled Feta cheese

Preheat oven to 350°. Spread pine nuts on a baking sheet and toast until golden, about 5-6 minutes. Remove from oven and set aside.

If using fresh beets, peel and slice beets. Cook in boiling water until tender; drain, rinse in cool water, drain again and set aside.

Make vinaigrette dressing by combining olive oil, vinegar, maple syrup, mustard and salt and blending until smooth.

Place spinach in a large salad bowl, pour dressing over and toss to coat. Divide spinach among 4-6 salad plates. Top with sliced beets, cheese and pine nuts.

Serve with:
Chicken Marsala
Category A items of your choice
If you are not serving with meat, Category B items of your choice
If you are serving with meat, Category C items of your choice

Spring Greens with Beets & Goat Cheese   Category: A   **Serves: 4-6**

2/3 cup pecan halves
3 tablespoons Balsamic vinegar, divided
1 tablespoon water
1 tablespoon sugar
1/4 cup olive oil
2 tablespoons maple syrup
1 teaspoon whole grain mustard
1/8 teaspoon salt
1-5 oz. package spring mix salad greens
1 lb. fresh beets, or 1-14 1/2 oz. can sliced beets, drained
1 cup crumbled goat cheese

In a large heavy skillet, cook the pecans, water and 1 tablespoon of the vinegar over medium heat until nuts are toasted, about 4 minutes. Sprinkle with sugar. Cook and stir for 2-4 minutes or until sugar is melted. Spread on foil to cool.

If using fresh beets, peel and slice beets. Cook in boiling water until tender; drain, rinse in cool water, drain again and set aside.

For dressing, in a small bowl, combine the oil, maple syrup, mustard, salt and remaining vinegar. Refrigerate until serving.

In a large bowl, combine salad greens and prepared dressing; toss to coat. Divide among eight salad plates. Top with beets, goat cheese and glazed pecans.

Serve with:
Category A items of your choice
If you are not serving with meat, *Sunflower Seed Bread* or other Category B items of your choice
If you are serving with meat, Category C items of your choice

Quinoa and Black Bean Salad   **Category: B**   **Serves: 4-6**

1 cup quinoa
2 cups water
1/2 cup olive oil
2 tablespoons fresh lime juice
2 teaspoons ground cumin
1/2 teaspoon ground coriander
2 tablespoons finely chopped fresh cilantro
2 tablespoons scallions
1-15 oz. can black beans, drained
1 cup diced tomatoes
1 cup diced roasted red pepper
1 tablespoon fresh green chilies
Salt and freshly ground black pepper

Put the quinoa in a mesh strainer and rinse well under cool running water.

Bring the water to a boil in a medium-sized saucepan. Add the quinoa, cover, and simmer on low heat for 10-15 minutes, or until all of the water is absorbed and the quinoa is tender. Allow it to cool for 15 minutes.

In a large bowl, combine the oil, lime juice, cumin, coriander, cilantro, and scallions.

Stir in the beans, tomatoes, red pepper, and chilies. Add the cooled quinoa. Season with salt and pepper to taste, and combine thoroughly. Refrigerate until ready to serve.

Serve with:
Sourdough Bread
Category A items of your choice
Category B items of your choice

Black Bean Asparagus Salad   **Category: A/B**   **Serves: 4-6**

1 lb. fresh asparagus, trimmed and cut into 1-inch pieces
1-15 oz. can black beans, rinsed and drained
1 medium sweet red pepper, cut into 1/2 inch pieces
1 tablespoon finely chopped onion
1/2 cup olive oil
2 tablespoons apple cider vinegar
1 tablespoon minced fresh cilantro
1 garlic clove, minced
1/2 teaspoon salt
1/2 teaspoon ground cumin
Dash of pepper

Place 1/2 inch of water in a large saucepan; add the asparagus. Bring to a boil. Reduce the heat; cover and simmer for 4-5 minutes or until crisp-tender. Drain.

In a bowl, combine the asparagus, beans, red pepper and onion. In a small bowl, whisk the oil, apple cider vinegar, cilantro, garlic, salt, cumin and pepper. Pour over the vegetables and toss to coat. Cover and refrigerate for at least 2 hours before serving.

<u>Serve with:</u>
Category A items of your choice
Category B items of your choice

Macaroni Salad   **Category: B**   **Serves: 10-12**

1 lb. gluten free macaroni
2 cups mayonnaise
1/2 cup gluten free salad dressing
1/3 cup chopped onions
2 teaspoons salt
10 hard boiled eggs (8 chopped; 2 sliced)
1 teaspoon paprika

Cook macaroni for 10–12 minutes in boiling water. Drain, rinse, drain again and place in large bowl.

In a medium sized bowl, stir together remaining ingredients except sliced eggs and paprika; add to macaroni and fold gently.

Top with egg slices and paprika. Cover and chill.

Serve with:
Category A items of your choice
Category B items of your choice

Potato Salad   **Category: B**   **Serves: 10-12**

10-12 medium to large potatoes
2 cups mayonnaise
1/2 cup salad dressing
1/3 cup chopped onions
2 teaspoons salt
10 hard boiled eggs (8 chopped; 2 sliced)
1 teaspoon paprika

Cook potatoes in boiling water with skin, covered, about 25 minutes. Drain and let cool for 30 minutes or until they reach room temperature. (You can speed along process by refrigerating them).

Peel and cube potatoes and place in large bowl.

In a medium sized bowl, stir together remaining ingredients except sliced eggs and paprika; add to potatoes and fold gently.

Top with egg slices and paprika. Cover and chill.

Serve with:
Category A items of your choice
Category B items of your choice

Colorful Bean Salad   **Category: A**   **Serves: 4-6**

3/4 lb. green beans, trimmed
3/4 lb. yellow wax beans, trimmed
1 lb. cherry tomatoes, halved
1 medium red onion, thinly sliced
1/2 cup thinly sliced fresh basil
1/2 cup extra-virgin olive oil
4 tablespoons red wine vinegar
1/4 teaspoon sugar
Salt and ground black pepper to taste

Cook green and yellow beans together in large pot of boiling salted water until crisp-tender, about 5 minutes. Drain; rinse with cold water and drain again. Set aside.

Combine beans, tomatoes, onion and basil in serving bowl. Whisk oil, vinegar and sugar in small bowl to blend. Season dressing with salt and pepper to taste. Pour dressing over vegetables; toss to coat.

Cover and chill at least 1 hour. Serve cold or at room temperature.

Variation: Use a mixture of red cherry tomatoes and golden cherry tomatoes for even more color.

Serve with:
Category A items of your choice
Category B items of your choice OR
Lamb and Zucchini Kebabs with Feta Sauce or other Category C items of your choice

Arugula Salad with Garlic Balsamic Vinaigrette   Category: A   Serves 4-6

For the vinaigrette:
2 garlic cloves
1/4 teaspoon salt
1 tablespoon minced shallots
2 tablespoons Balsamic vinegar
1/4 cup extra-virgin olive oil

For the salad:
3 bunches arugula
1 pint cherry tomatoes, halved
1 carrot, peeled and shredded
Salt and ground black pepper to taste

Finely mince garlic. In a bowl whisk together garlic, salt, shallots, vinegar and oil.

Trim stems from arugula and tear leaves in half. In a bowl toss together arugula, tomatoes, and carrot.

Just before serving, drizzle vinaigrette over salad and toss with salt and pepper to taste.

Serve with:
Category A items of your choice
Multi Grain Bread or other Category B items of your choice OR
Category C items of your choice

Classic Chicken Salad   **Category: C**   **Serves: 4**

2 very large whole, bone-in, chicken breasts with skin
2 tablespoons extra-virgin olive oil
Salt
2 stalks celery, diced
2 green onions, white and green parts only, sliced thinly
1 cup mayonnaise
1 tablespoon fresh lemon juice
2 tablespoons chopped fresh parsley
Salt and ground black pepper to taste

Heat oven to 400º. Place chicken breasts on a baking dish, rub with oil and sprinkle with salt. Roast until done, about 35-40 minutes. Remove from pan and set aside to cool.

When chicken breasts are cool, remove skin and bones and discard. Chop or shred meat into bite-sized pieces.

Combine chicken, celery, onions, mayonnaise, lemon juice and parsley in a large bowl; stir to combine. Add salt and pepper to taste, stir again and serve.

Serve with:
Category A items of your choice
Category C items of your choice

Scrumptious Steak Salad   **Category: A/C**   **Serves: 2-3**

For spice mix:
1 tablespoon paprika
2 teaspoons ground black pepper
1 1/2 teaspoons salt
2 teaspoons garlic powder
1/2 teaspoon cayenne pepper
1 teaspoon dried oregano
1 teaspoon dried thyme leaves

For salad dressing:
1/4 cup olive oil
2 tablespoons Balsamic vinegar or red wine vinegar
1 teaspoon Dijon mustard
Salt and ground black pepper to taste

For salad:
6 cups mixed salad greens of your choice
1/2 green bell pepper, thinly sliced
1/2 red bell pepper, thinly sliced
1 medium cucumber, thinly sliced
1/2 cup thinly sliced red onion

2 5-6 oz. beef tenderloin steaks
3 tablespoons butter or Earth Balance, melted
6 tablespoons crumbled blue cheese (about 3 oz.) or Feta cheese
1 tomato, chopped

Combine all spice mix ingredients in small bowl.

Whisk oil, vinegar and mustard in large bowl to blend. Season to taste with salt and pepper. Add greens, bell peppers, cucumber and onion and toss to coat. Divide salad between 2 or 3 plates.

Spread spice mixture on plate. Dip steaks in melted butter then press to coat both sides of steaks with spice mixture.

Heat heavy, large skillet over high heat until very hot. Add steaks and cook to desired doneness, about 2 minutes per side for medium-rare. Transfer to cutting board and let cool for 2-3 minutes.

Thinly slice steaks crosswise and arrange slices atop salads. Sprinkle with cheese, garnish with chopped tomato and serve.

<u>Serve with:</u>
Category A items of your choice
Category C items of your choice

Soups

Spicy Black Bean Vegetable Soup   **Category: B**   **Serves: 4**

4 tablespoons extra virgin olive oil
1 large or 2 small onions, diced
3 stalks celery, sliced
5 carrots, peeled and sliced
4 cloves garlic, minced
4 cups vegetable broth or stock
2-15 oz. cans black beans, rinsed and drained
2 medium tomatoes, diced
1 heaping tablespoon ground cumin
1/2 teaspoon chili powder
Dash cayenne pepper
1 medium yellow (summer) squash, diced
1 medium zucchini squash, diced
Chopped fresh cilantro, parsley or basil for garnish (optional)
Sour cream for garnish (optional)

Heat the oil in a Dutch oven over medium heat. Sauté onion, carrots and celery about 5 minutes. Add garlic and sauté 2 minutes more, being careful not to let it brown.

Add cumin, chili powder and cayenne and stir to combine. Add broth, beans and tomatoes. Bring to a boil, reduce heat and simmer 15 minutes.

Stir in yellow squash and zucchini and simmer 5 minutes more or until squash is just tender (do not overcook).

Serve topped with cilantro, parsley, basil and/or sour cream if desired.

Serve with:
Cornbread
Category A items of your choice
Category B items of your choice

Cabbage Soup   **Category: C**   **Serves: 6**

1 lb. ground beef or ground turkey
1 clove garlic, minced
2 stalks of celery, chopped
1 medium onion, chopped
1-15 oz. can red kidney beans, rinsed and drained
1-28 oz. can crushed tomatoes
1-28 oz. can water (use tomato can)
4 gluten free beef, chicken or vegetable bouillon cubes
1 small head green cabbage, shredded
Salt and pepper to taste
Sour cream for garnish (optional)

Brown the beef or turkey and drain the grease.

Put all ingredients in large soup pot, bring to a boil and simmer about 1 hour or until cabbage is done.

Serve topped with sour cream if desired.

Serve with:
Category A items of your choice
Category C items of your choice

Seafood Chowder   **Category: C**   **Serves: 6-8**

1/2 teaspoon butter or Earth Balance
2 slices bacon, minced
1 cup onion, minced
1 cup celery, chopped
3 cloves garlic, minced or pressed
2-14 1/2 oz. cans chicken broth
1/2 teaspoon dried thyme
1/4 teaspoon salt
1/4 teaspoon pepper
1 teaspoon dried parsley flakes
2 cups cauliflower, cut into small pieces
3 cups broccoli florets cut into small pieces
1 lb. scallops
1 1/2 tablespoons corn starch
1-8 oz. bottle clam juice
1 1/2 cups half-and-half
1/2 lb. crab meat
1 lb. fresh shrimp, shelled and deveined
1/2 cup sherry
1/2 cup grated Romano cheese

In a large sauce pan, melt the butter and sauté the bacon bits over medium-high heat. When the bacon is crisp, add the celery and onion and continue to cook, stirring frequently until the vegetables are tender; about 5 minutes. Add garlic and cook for 1 minute.

Add the chicken broth and bring it to a boil.

Add the thyme, salt, pepper, parsley flakes, cauliflower and broccoli; simmer 5 minutes.

In a medium bowl, whisk the corn starch into the clam juice. Add this mixture to the vegetables in the sauce pan and bring to a boil. Reduce the heat, stir in the half-and-half and simmer for 10 minutes.

Stir in the scallops, shrimp, crab meat, sherry, and cheese. Cook the chowder over low heat until the cheese is melted.

Remove from heat and set the chowder aside for 1 hour, covered, to allow the flavors to blend well and seafood to finish cooking. Place the pan back over low heat to slowly reheat it. Do not allow it to boil.

<u>Serve with:</u>
Category A items of your choice
Category C items of your choice

Loaded Minestrone Soup   **Category: B**   **Serves: 10-12**

1/4 cup olive oil
2 cloves garlic, minced
1 large onion, diced
3 celery stalks, sliced
14 cups beef broth or stock, or vegetable broth or stock
1 cup dried split peas
1 cup dried lentils
4 large carrots, peeled and sliced
1-28 oz. can crushed tomatoes
2-15 oz. cans cannellini beans, rinsed and drained
1-15 oz. can of garbanzo beans, rinsed and drained
1-15 oz. can of red kidney beans, rinsed and drained
1 medium zucchini, diced
1 medium yellow squash, diced
1/2 lb. fresh green beans cut into 1/2 inch pieces
1 lb. escarole, rinsed and chopped
Salt and ground black pepper to taste
1/2 cup grated Parmesan cheese

In a 16 quart soup or stock pot, heat the oil over medium-high heat. Add the garlic, onion, and celery; sauté until softened. Add the broth or stock and bring to a boil. Add split peas and lentils; return to a boil. Reduce heat to low and simmer for 30 minutes.

Add the carrots and tomatoes; continue to simmer for 20 minutes. Add the drained cannellini, garbanzo, and kidney beans; then the zucchini, yellow squash, green beans and escarole. Simmer for 10 minutes or until all vegetables are tender.

Season with salt and pepper, and serve with cheese.

Serve with:
Herbed Italian Bread or other gluten free bread of your choice
Category A items of your choice
Category B items of your choice

**Yellow Tomato Soup with Goat
Cheese Croutons**   **Category: A/B**   **Serves 6**

3 lbs. yellow tomatoes, halved (about 9 medium)
2 tablespoons olive oil, divided
4 garlic cloves, minced, divided
1 teaspoon salt
1 teaspoon pepper
1 teaspoon minced fresh rosemary
1 teaspoon minced fresh thyme
1 large onion, chopped
1 cup vegetable broth or stock
1/2 cup milk
1/2 cup heavy whipping cream

Croutons (optional):

12 slices gluten free French bread (1/2 inch thick)
1 tablespoon olive oil
2 tablespoons *Basil Pesto* (see page 66) or prepared gluten free pesto
1/2 cup crumbled goat cheese
1 teaspoon ground black pepper

Place tomatoes, cut side down, in a greased 15 inch x 10 inch x 1 inch baking pan; brush with 1 tablespoon oil. Sprinkle with 2 teaspoons garlic and the salt, pepper, rosemary and thyme.

Bake at 400° for 25-30 minutes or until tomatoes are tender and skins are charred. Cool slightly. Discard tomato skins. In a blender, process the tomatoes until blended.

In a large saucepan, sauté onion in remaining oil until tender. Add remaining garlic; sauté 1 minute longer. Stir in broth and milk; bring to a boil. Carefully stir in tomato purée. Simmer, uncovered, for 15 minutes to allow flavors to blend. Stir in cream; heat through (do not boil).

Meanwhile, if using croutons, place bread on a baking sheet and brush with oil. Bake 5-6 minutes or until golden brown. Spread with pesto and sprinkle with goat cheese and pepper. Bake additional 2 minutes.

Ladle soup into bowls and top with croutons.

Serve with:
Brown Bread or other gluten free bread of your choice
Category A items of your choice
Category B items of your choice

French Onion Soup   **Category: A/C**   **Serves 6**

For the soup:
4 tablespoons unsalted butter
5 medium red onions (about 3 lbs.), peeled and sliced thin
1/2 teaspoon salt
6 cups low-sodium chicken broth or stock
1 3/4 cups low-sodium beef broth or stock
1/4 cup dry red wine
3 sprigs fresh parsley
1 sprig fresh thyme
1 bay leaf
1 tablespoon Balsamic vinegar
Salt and ground black pepper to taste

For the cheese topping:
6 thick slices gluten-free bread
1/4 lb. Swiss cheese, sliced
1 1/2 cups grated Asiago cheese

Melt butter in a large stockpot or soup pot over medium-high heat. Add sliced onions and 1/2 teaspoon salt; stir to coat onions with butter. Cook, stirring frequently until the onions are brown and caramelized and the bottom of the pot is coated with a deep brown crust; about 30-35 minutes.

Stir in the chicken and beef broths, red wine, parsley, thyme and bay leaf, scraping the bottom of the pot to loosen the browned bits and bring to a simmer. Simmer for 20 minutes and then discard the herbs. Stir in vinegar and add salt and pepper to taste. Keep hot.

Adjust oven rack to the upper-middle position and preheat broiler. Place heat-safe soup bowls or crocks on a baking sheet and fill each with about 1 1/2 cups soup. Top each with a slice of gluten-free bread, sliced Swiss cheese and then about 2 tablespoons Asiago cheese.

Broil until well-browned and bubbly, about 10 minutes. Cool 3-4 minutes and serve.

<u>Serve with:</u>
Pumpernickel Bread
Category A items of your choice

Potato-Leek Soup   **Category: B**   **Serves: 6-8**

4 1/2 lbs. leeks
8 tablespoons (1 stick) unsalted butter
1 tablespoon gluten free flour
5 1/2 cups chicken broth or vegetable broth
1 bay leaf
2 lbs. red potatoes (about 6 medium), scrubbed and cut into 3/4 inch pieces
Salt and ground black pepper to taste

Cut off the roots and upper dark green portions of the leeks, leaving the white portion and about 3 inches of the light green portion. Slice the leeks in half lengthwise and then slice each half crosswise into 1-inch pieces.

Place leeks into a large colander or strainer and immerse colander into a sink full of cold water to draw out sand. Soak leeks 5 minutes, remove the colander from the sink and drain water. Rinse sand from sink and repeat soaking process until all sand is removed. Rinse leeks, drain and set aside.

Heat butter in a large soup pot or Dutch oven over medium-low heat until foaming. Stir in leeks, cover and cook until leeks are tender, about 15-20 minutes. Sprinkle flour over leeks and stir to blend.

Increase heat to high and gradually add the broth, whisking constantly to prevent lumping. Add the potatoes and bay leaf and bring to a boil. Cover, reduce heat to low and simmer 5-7 minutes, until potatoes are almost tender.

Remove pot from heat and let stand, covered until the potatoes are tender and the flavors have blended, about 15 minutes.

Remove bay leaf, add salt and pepper to taste and serve.

Serve with:
Cheesy Onion Bread
Category A items of your choice
Category B items of your choice

Lentil Soup   **Category: B**   **Serves: 6**

3 cups dry green lentils
7 cups vegetable broth or stock
1 teaspoon salt
8 cloves garlic, crushed
1 large Vidalia onion, chopped
3 stalks celery, sliced
3 carrots, peeled and sliced
1 tablespoon chopped fresh basil (or 1 teaspoon dried basil)
1/2 teaspoon dried thyme leaves
1 teaspoon dried oregano
Ground black pepper to taste
3 medium ripe tomatoes, diced (or 1-28oz. can diced tomatoes, undrained)

Place lentils, broth and salt in a Dutch oven or soup pot. Bring to a boil over high heat, reduce heat to low and simmer, partially covered, for 30 minutes. Add garlic, onion, celery, carrots, basil, thyme, oregano and pepper; simmer partially covered for an additional 15 minutes.

Stir in tomatoes and cook 10 minutes more, or until all vegetables and lentils are tender.

Serve with:
Gluten free bread of your choice
Category A items of your choice
Category B items of your choice

Roasted Winter Vegetable Soup   **Category: B**   **Serves: 6**

5 tablespoons butter or Earth Balance, divided
1 2- lb. butternut squash, unpeeled, halved lengthwise, seeded, cut into 8 pieces
1 lb. parsnips, peeled, cut crosswise into 2-inch pieces, thick end pieces cut lengthwise in half
3 carrots, peeled and cut lengthwise into 3 pieces
1/4 cup water
1 large onion, halved, thinly sliced
2 teaspoons minced fresh thyme or 3/4 teaspoon dried thyme
4 1/2 cups chicken broth or stock
1 cup half and half or light cream
Salt and ground black pepper to taste

Preheat oven to 375°. Grease large roasting pan with 1 tablespoon of the butter. Arrange squash pieces, skin side up, in prepared roasting pan. Add parsnips, carrots and water to pan. Cover with foil and bake until vegetables are very tender, about 50 minutes. Set aside and cool.

While vegetables are roasting, melt remaining 4 tablespoons butter in large skillet over medium-low heat. Add onion and thyme; sauté until onion is tender and golden, about 10 minutes. Remove from heat.

Scrape squash pulp from skin and place into food processor. Add parsnips, carrots and onion mixture. Purée until smooth.

Transfer puréed mixture to large saucepan and stir in chicken broth. Whisk in half and half.   Bring to simmer over medium-low heat. Season with salt and pepper and serve.

Serve with:
Sourdough Brown Bread
Category A items of your choice
Category B items of your choice

Easy Chicken Vegetable Soup   Category: C   Serves: 6

6 cups chicken broth or stock
1 1/2 lbs. skinless boneless chicken breasts
1 medium onion, chopped
4 tablespoons olive oil
3 garlic cloves, minced
4 carrots, peeled and cut diagonally into 1/3-inch slices
3 stalks celery, cut crosswise into 1/3-inch slices
1 medium zucchini, quartered lengthwise and each quarter cut crosswise into 1/2-inch slices
1 teaspoon salt
1/4 teaspoon ground black pepper
3 tablespoons finely chopped fresh parsley

Bring broth to a simmer in a large saucepan. Add chicken and simmer, uncovered, 5 minutes. Remove pan from heat and cover, then let stand until chicken is cooked through, about 8-10 minutes (do not overcook). Transfer chicken to a plate and cool, reserving poaching liquid. Cut chicken into bite-sized pieces.

Cook onion in oil in a soup pot or Dutch oven over medium heat, stirring occasionally, until softened but not browned, about 6 minutes. Add garlic and cook until fragrant, about 1 minute. Add carrots, celery, salt, and pepper and cook, covered, stirring occasionally, until softened, 8 to 10 minutes.

Add reserved poaching liquid and simmer, covered, for 8 minutes. Add zucchini and continue to simmer another 5 minutes or until vegetables are tender but not mushy. Remove from heat.

Stir cut up chicken into soup along with parsley; serve immediately.

Serve with:
Category A items of your choice
Category C items of your choice

Pasta E Fagioli   **Category: B**   **Serves: 6**

3-15 oz. cans Great Northern or Cannellini beans, rinsed and drained, divided
1/4 cup olive oil
1 large Vidalia onion, chopped
2 carrots, diced
2 stalks celery, sliced
4 cloves garlic, minced
1/2 cup chopped fresh parsley
1/4 cup chopped fresh basil leaves
8 cups vegetable broth
6 tablespoons tomato paste
Salt and ground black pepper to taste
3 cups cooked small gluten-free pasta, such as elbows, shells or bowties
1/2 cup grated Parmesan or Romano cheese, plus more for garnish

Drain and rinse one of the cans of beans and mash thoroughly or purée in a blender. Set aside. Drain and rinse other two cans of beans and set aside.

Heat oil in a Dutch oven or soup pot over medium heat and sauté onion 5 minutes. Add carrots, celery, garlic, parsley and basil and cook another 8-10 minutes. Stir in broth, mashed or puréed beans, whole beans and tomato paste. Bring to a boil over high heat, then reduce heat, cover and simmer for 30 minutes or until carrots and celery are tender.

Stir in gluten-free pasta and cook just long enough to heat pasta through, about 2-3 minutes. If soup seems too thick, add a little extra water or vegetable broth. Stir in cheese.

Top with additional Parmesan or Romano cheese if desired.

Note: To prevent pasta from getting too soft if there are leftovers, instead of adding pasta to soup while cooking, you can keep them separate and just add pasta to individual bowls as the soup is served.

<u>Serve with:</u>
Roasted Garlic Bread
Category A items of your choice
Category B items of your choice

Entrees

Chicken Marsala   **Category: C**   **Serves: 4**

1 3/4 cups reduced sodium chicken broth or stock
2 tablespoons finely chopped shallots
3 tablespoons unsalted butter
10 oz. mushrooms, trimmed and thinly sliced
1 1/2 teaspoons finely chopped fresh sage
1/4 teaspoon salt
1/8 teaspoon ground black pepper
4 skinless boneless chicken breast halves (2 lbs. total)
Salt, ground black pepper and garlic powder for seasoning chicken
1/4 cup extra virgin olive oil
1/2 cup plus 2 tablespoons dry Marsala wine
2/3 cup heavy cream
1 teaspoon fresh lemon juice

Bring broth to a boil in 2 quart sauce pan over high heat, then boil, uncovered, until reduced to about 3/4 cup; about 20 minutes.

Cook shallots in butter in an 8 to 10 inch heavy skillet over moderate heat, stirring, until shallots begin to turn golden; about 1 minute. Add mushrooms, 1 teaspoon sage, salt, and pepper and cook stirring occasionally, until the liquid the mushrooms give off is evaporated and mushrooms begin to brown; about 6-8 minutes. Remove from heat.

Heat olive oil in a 10 inch heavy skillet over medium-high heat. Sprinkle chicken generously with salt, pepper and garlic powder. Cook chicken, turning once, until golden and just cooked through; about 8-10 minutes (do not overcook). Transfer cooked chicken to a plate; cover and keep warm.

Add 1/2 cup of wine to chicken skillet and boil over high heat, stirring and scraping up the browned bits; about 30 seconds. Add reduced broth, cream, and mushrooms then simmer, stirring occasionally, until sauce is slightly thickened, 10-12 minutes. Stir in lemon juice and remaining 2 tablespoons wine and 1/2 teaspoon sage. Serve chicken with sauce.

<u>Serve with:</u>
Spinach Salad with Beets & Feta Cheese or Tossed Salad
Roasted Broccoli
Category A items of your choice

Goat Cheese Quesadillas with Roasted Red Pepper Sauce   **Category: B**   **Serves: 3-4**

1 small onion, coarsely chopped
3 garlic cloves, chopped
3 tablespoons olive oil, divided
2 red bell peppers, roasted (instructions below)
2 tablespoons chopped fresh basil leaves
Salt and ground black pepper to taste
Six 9-10 inch gluten free flour tortillas
1-8 oz. log soft mild goat cheese, cut into 4 pieces, at room temperature
1/4 cup *Basil Pesto* (see page 66) or prepared gluten free pesto
1 small onion, sliced thin
2 tablespoons unsalted butter, softened

Sauce:
In a skillet cook onion and garlic in 2 tablespoons oil over moderate heat, stirring, until softened. Transfer onion mixture to a food processor and add roasted peppers, basil, remaining 1 tablespoon oil and salt and pepper to taste. Blend sauce until smooth and transfer to small bowl. (Sauce may be made up to 3 days ahead and chilled, covered.)

Put 1 tortilla on a work surface and spread with 1 goat cheese piece, covering surface evenly. Spread 1 tablespoon pesto over goat cheese and cover with one fourth of onion. Repeat layering in the same manner, ending with a tortilla and gently pressing layers together. Make 1 more layered quesadilla with remaining tortillas, goat cheese, pesto, and onion. Spread top and bottom of each quesadilla with 1/2 tablespoon butter.

Heat a griddle or well seasoned 10 inch cast-iron skillet over medium heat until hot but not smoking. Cook quesadillas, one at a time, gently pressing down with a metal spatula, until golden; about 4 minutes on each side. Cut each quesadilla into 8 wedges and serve warm with roasted red pepper sauce.

To Roast Peppers:
Using a long handled fork, carefully char peppers over an open flame or on a rack set over an electric burner, turning them until their skins are blackened; 4-6 minutes. (Or broil peppers on a rack of a broiler about 2 inches from heat, turning them every 5 minutes, for about 15-20 minutes, or until skins are

blistered and charred.) Transfer peppers to a bowl and let stand, covered, until cool enough to handle. Peel peppers, cut off tops and discard seeds and ribs.

<u>Serve with:</u>
Tossed Salad
Category A items of your choice

Macaroni and Cheese   **Category: B**   **Serves: 2-4**

2 cups (8 oz.) gluten free elbow macaroni
8 tablespoons (1 stick) butter or Earth Balance, divided
1/4 cup onion, finely diced
3 tablespoons gluten free flour
2 cups milk or light cream
1/2 cup dry white wine (or water)
2 cups grated sharp Cheddar cheese (about 1/2 lb.)
1/2 cup gluten free bread crumbs (for topping)
Salt and fresh ground black pepper
Cayenne pepper to taste
1/2 teaspoon paprika

Preheat oven to 350°.

Bring 4 quarts salted water to a rapid boil and cook the macaroni until not quite tender. Drain and set aside.

Breadcrumb topping:
In small frying pan or sauté pan, melt 1/2 stick (4 tablespoons) of butter. Stir in the breadcrumbs and toast just until lightly browned. Remove from heat and set aside.

In medium saucepan, melt remaining butter, add onions, and stir over low heat until the onions are just translucent, but not browned. Stir in the flour and seasonings. Continue to cook for an additional 2-3 minutes. Add the wine (or water), then gradually stir in the milk (or cream).

Simmer over low heat, stirring constantly until the sauce is thickened and smooth. Add cheese and continue stirring until the cheese melts.

In a large bowl, combine the macaroni with the cheese sauce. Turn out into a generously buttered casserole dish (approximately 1 1/2 quarts). Sprinkle with breadcrumb topping.

Bake for approximately 20 minutes or until heated through and golden on top.

<u>Serve with:</u>
Tossed Salad
Roasted Asparagus
Category A items of your choice

Spinach and Ricotta Pasta   **Category: B**   **Serves: 2–4**

1-8 oz. package gluten free pasta (penne pasta works well for this recipe)
1-10 oz. package frozen chopped spinach, thawed and well drained
3 tablespoons olive oil
3 tablespoons butter
3 cloves garlic, minced
2 tablespoons chopped fresh parsley (or 1 1/2 teaspoons dried parsley)
1 1/2 teaspoons oregano
1/2 cup grated Parmesan or Romano cheese
1 cup Ricotta cheese
Salt and ground black pepper to taste

Cook pasta until tender; drain and set aside.

In a large skillet, sauté oil, butter and garlic over medium heat until garlic is fragrant.

Add spinach, cheeses, parsley, oregano and cooked pasta to pan; sprinkle with salt and pepper to taste. Cook over medium-low heat until warmed through.

Serve immediately.

Serve with:
Tomato Rosemary Bread
Tossed Salad
Category A items of your choice

Artichoke Quiche   **Category: C**   **Serves: 4-6**

1-12oz. jar artichoke hearts, drained
1/4 cup fresh mushrooms, sliced
1 tablespoon butter
2 cups shredded Parmesan, Swiss or Cheddar cheese (or a mixture of each)
4 eggs, beaten
1 cup milk
1/2 cup chopped onion
1/2 teaspoon pepper
1/4 teaspoon basil

Preheat oven to 350°. Lightly grease a 9 inch pie plate or quiche dish.

Roughly chop artichokes and place in bottom of dish. In a small skillet, sauté mushrooms and onions in butter until onions are translucent. Pour over artichokes. Sprinkle with shredded cheese. In a separate bowl, whisk together eggs, milk, pepper and basil. Pour into pie plate.

Bake 30-40 minutes or until the center of quiche is firm.

Serve with:
Tossed salad
Roasted Brussels Sprouts
Category A items of your choice
Category C items of your choice

Curried Eggplant with   Category: A/B   Serves: 2-4
Chickpeas and Spinach

2 large garlic cloves, minced
Pinch salt
2 teaspoons curry powder
1/2 cup olive oil
1 medium eggplant (about 1 1/2 lbs.) peeled and cut into 3/4 inch pieces
1 large onion, cut into 1/2 inch wedges
1-15 oz. can chickpeas, rinsed and drained
2 tablespoons finely julienned fresh ginger
Freshly ground black pepper
1-5 oz. bag fresh baby spinach
Plain yogurt or sour cream for serving

Preheat oven to 425°.

On a work surface or small plate, mash the garlic with a pinch of salt to a paste consistency.

In a large roasting pan, mix the garlic paste with the curry powder and olive oil. Add the eggplant, onion, chickpeas and ginger, season with salt and pepper and toss well. Spread the vegetables in an even layer and roast for about 30 minutes, stirring once or twice, until the eggplant and onion are tender.

Stir in the spinach and roast just until wilted; about 2 minutes.

Serve topped with plain yogurt or sour cream.

Serve with:
Gluten free flat bread
Cooked gluten free pasta
Category A items of your choice
Category B items of your choice

White Bean Stew with Swiss Chard **Category: A/B** **Serves: 4**
and Tomatoes

2 lbs. Swiss chard, tough stems discarded and leaves cut crosswise into 2 inch strips
1/4 cup extra virgin olive oil
3 cloves garlic, thinly sliced
1/4 teaspoon crushed red pepper
1-14 oz. can diced tomatoes
2-16 oz. cans Cannellini beans, rinsed and drained
Salt to taste

Bring a soup pot or large sauce pan of water to a boil. Add the Swiss chard and simmer over moderate heat until tender; about 8 minutes. Drain and gently press out excess water.

In the sauce pan, heat the oil. Add the garlic and crushed red pepper and cook over moderately high heat until the garlic is golden; about 1 minute.

Add the tomatoes and bring to a boil. Add the beans and simmer over moderately high heat for 3 minutes. Add the chard and simmer over moderate heat until the flavors blend; about 5 minutes. Season the stew with salt to taste, and serve.

Serve with:
Tomato Rosemary Bread or other gluten free bread of your choice
Cooked gluten free pasta
Category A items of your choice
Category B items of your choice

Chicken and Andouille Gumbo   **Category: C**   **Serves: 6**

1/2 cup all-purpose gluten free flour
1 tablespoon olive oil
1 link (3 1/2 oz.) Andouille sausage, finely chopped
3 medium celery stalks, cut into 1/2 inch chunks.
1 large onion, cut into 1/2 inch chunks
1 large green bell pepper, cut into 1/2 inch chunks
12 oz. okra, trimmed and sliced crosswise, 1/2 inch thick
8 cups low-sodium chicken broth or stock
8 skinless chicken thighs (about 2 lbs.)
1-28 oz. can plum tomatoes with juice, coarsely chopped (should be 2 cups-add water if needed)
2 bay leaves
1 tablespoon gluten free Worcestershire sauce

Heat a large skillet over medium-high heat. Toast flour, stirring with a wooden spoon, for 3 minutes. Reduce heat to medium; cook, stirring to break up any lumps, until it reaches the color of peanut butter and has a toasted aroma, about 14 minutes more. (Lower heat to prevent burning.) Transfer to a large bowl; let cool.

Heat oil in a large pot or Dutch oven over medium heat. Cook sausage for 1 minute. Raise heat to high. Add celery, onion, and bell pepper. Cook, stirring occasionally, until slightly soft, about 4 minutes. Add okra; cook for 3 minutes.

Meanwhile, gradually whisk stock into flour; add to pot. Stir in chicken, tomatoes, and bay leaves; bring to a boil. Reduce heat to medium; simmer for 1 hour.

Remove from heat, transfer chicken to a plate and cover soup to keep warm. Let chicken cool for 5 minutes. Remove meat from bones; shred or chop, and return to pot. Discard bones and bay leaves. Stir in Worcestershire sauce.

Serve with:
Category A items of your choice
Category C items of your choice

Lamb and Zucchini Kebabs   Category: C   Serves: 4
with Feta Sauce

For the Kebabs:
1/2 cup extra virgin olive oil
1/2 teaspoon finely grated lemon zest
1/4 cup fresh lemon juice
1 lemon, cut into 8 wedges
3 cloves garlic, minced
2 teaspoons oregano
1/2 boneless leg of lamb (3 1/2 lbs.), cut into 1 1/2 inch cubes
1 large zucchini, halved lengthwise and cut into 24 pieces
2 red peppers, seeded and each cut into 12 chunks (for a total of 24 chunks)
1 large onion, cut into 24 wedges
Salt and freshly ground black pepper

For the Feta Sauce:
2/3 cup Feta cheese, crumbled
1/2 cup Greek yogurt or plain yogurt
3 cloves garlic, minced
1/2 teaspoon oregano
3 tablespoons extra virgin olive oil
1 tablespoon fresh lemon juice

Prepare the lamb: Combine oil, lemon zest and juice, 3 cloves garlic, oregano, and lamb in a glass dish; marinate for 30 minutes.

Make the Feta sauce: Place all sauce ingredients in a food processor and process until very smooth.

Heat grill to a medium high heat or preheat oven broiler. Thread lamb, zucchini, peppers and onion onto 8 skewers, ending each with a lemon wedge. Season with salt and pepper. Grill or broil 10-12 minutes or until medium rare, turning halfway through. Serve with Feta sauce.

<u>Serve with:</u>
Colorful Bean Salad
Category A items of your choice
Category C items of your choice

Gluten Free Pasta and Vodka Sauce   **Category: B**   **Serves: 4-6**

For the sauce:
3 tablespoons butter
3 large cloves garlic, finely chopped
2 tablespoons red onion, finely chopped
1-28 oz. can crushed tomatoes
1/2 teaspoon crushed red pepper (or more to taste)
2 tablespoons chopped fresh basil (or 1 teaspoon dried basil)
Salt and ground black pepper to taste
1/2 cup heavy cream
1/4 cup Vodka
1/2 cup fresh or frozen peas
1/2 cup grated Parmesan or Romano cheese

1 lb. gluten free pasta, cooked and drained, reserving 1 cup of cooking liquid

In a very large skillet or Dutch oven, melt butter over medium heat. Add garlic and onion and cook about 2 minutes.

Add tomatoes, crushed red pepper, basil, salt and pepper. Bring to a boil, reduce heat and simmer on low for 5 minutes.

Stir in the cream. Mix well and cook for about 3-4 minutes. Add the vodka, stir well and cook for 2 minutes. Add peas and simmer for another 10 minutes.

Add cooked pasta to the pan and toss until well coated. If sauce seems too thick, add small amounts of the pasta water until desired consistency. Stir in cheese and toss again. Serve immediately.

Serve with:
Tossed Salad
Gluten free bread of your choice
Category A items of your choice
Category B items of your choice

Gluten Free Pasta with   Category: B   Serves: 4-6
Cream of Pesto Sauce

Sauce ingredients:
2 tablespoons olive oil
1 small onion, chopped
8 cloves garlic, sliced thick
1/4 cup butter or Earth Balance
1/3 cup heavy cream
Pinch salt
Large pinch of crushed red pepper (only if NOT using the option of dried chili peppers below)
Pinch ground black pepper
1/4 teaspoon oregano
1 1/2 cups grated or shredded Romano cheese
1 cup *Basil Pesto* (see page 66) or prepared gluten free pesto

1 lb. gluten free pasta, cooked and drained

Optional ingredients:
10 sundried tomatoes packed in oil, sliced
5 crushed dried chili peppers
15 mushrooms, chopped

Heat olive oil in a large skillet and sauté onion until tender and translucent. Stir in garlic, butter and choice of red pepper or chili peppers. Sauté until garlic is soft and fragrant; about 1 minute.

Stir in heavy cream and seasonings, and simmer for 4-5 minutes stirring constantly. Add cheese and continue to stir until melted. Add pesto, and optional mushrooms and/or sundried tomatoes. Cook about 5 minutes, or until heated thoroughly. Combine pasta and sauce in a large bowl; toss to coat.

Serve with:
Tossed Salad
Gluten free bread of your choice
Category A items of your choice
Category B items of your choice

Salmon and Whitefish Cakes with   **Category: C**   **Serves: 4**
Horseradish Cucumber Sauce

Sauce ingredients:
1 cup finely chopped unpeeled cucumbers
3/4 cup mayonnaise
3 tablespoons prepared white horseradish (you may add more later for desired heat)
2 tablespoons finely chopped fresh parsley
1 tablespoon finely chopped fresh chives
Salt and ground black pepper to taste

Fish cakes:
3 tablespoons olive oil, plus more for frying fish cakes
3 medium carrots, peeled and finely chopped
1 stalk celery, finely chopped
1 cup chopped leeks or green onions (white and pale green parts only)
2 large eggs
6 tablespoons gluten free bread crumbs
1 1/4 teaspoons salt
3/4 teaspoon ground white pepper
1 lb. skinless whitefish fillet, cut into 1 inch cubes
1 lb. skinless salmon fillet, cut into 1 inch cubes
Lemon wedges
Fresh parsley sprigs

For Sauce: Stir cucumber, mayonnaise, horseradish, parsley, and chives in medium bowl to blend. Season sauce to taste with salt and pepper; add extra horseradish if desired. Cover and refrigerate.

Prepare Fish Cakes: Line work surface or large rimmed baking sheet with plastic wrap.

Heat 3 tablespoons of oil in a large heavy skillet over medium heat. Add carrots, celery and leeks or green onions. Sauté until soft but not brown; about 15 minutes. Remove from heat and set aside.

Beat eggs, bread crumbs, salt and white pepper in a large bowl to blend. Stir in sautéed vegetable mixture.

Place whitefish and salmon cubes into food processor. Pulse until fish is a coarse paste consistency (it is OK if small chunks of fish remain). Stir fish into bread crumb/vegetable mixture.

Using wet hands, take about 1/3 cup of the fish mixture for each cake, shape into sixteen 1/2 inch thick cakes and place on work surface covered with plastic wrap to avoid sticking to surface. (Note: These can be made the day before, put on a baking sheet lined with plastic wrap, covered and refrigerated.)

Add enough oil to 2 heavy skillets to coat bottoms. Heat the oil over medium-high heat. Add 8 fish cakes to each skillet, and sauté until golden and cooked through; about 3 minutes per side.

Serve with horseradish cucumber sauce over or alongside and garnish with lemon wedges and parsley.

Serve with:
Garlicky Green Beans with Arugula
Roasted Broccoli
Tossed Salad
Category A items of your choice

Chicken Louisa   **Category: C**   **Serves: 4**

4 (1/3 inch thick) chicken cutlets (about 1 1/2 lbs.)
Salt and ground black pepper to taste
1 tablespoon olive oil
1 tablespoon unsalted butter
1 medium shallot, finely chopped
1/2 cup dry white wine or dry vermouth
3/4 cup heavy cream
4 or 5 plum tomatoes, coarsely chopped
2 tablespoons finely chopped fresh tarragon (or 2 teaspoons dried tarragon)
1/2 extra large gluten free chicken bouillon cube, crumbled
Chopped fresh chives for garnish (optional)

Pat chicken dry with paper towels and season with salt and pepper. Heat oil and butter in a 12 inch heavy skillet over moderately high heat until foam subsides. Brown chicken on both sides in 2 batches, about 3 minutes per batch. Transfer chicken to a plate and keep warm.

Add shallot to skillet and cook, stirring, until tender; about 1 minute. Add wine and boil over high heat, scraping up brown bits until reduced by half. Stir in cream, tomatoes, tarragon, and bouillon cube, reduce heat and simmer until tomatoes are softened and sauce begins to thicken; about 3-4 minutes. Season to taste with salt and pepper.

Return chicken with the juices to the skillet and simmer until cooked through; about 4-5 minutes.

Garnish with finely chopped fresh chives if desired.

Serve with:
Italian Broccoli Rabe
Category A items of your choice
Category C items of your choice

Chicken Piccata   **Category: C**   **Serves: 6**

1/4 cup fresh lemon juice
1 lemon, sliced 1/4 inch thick
6 boneless, skinless chicken cutlets
Salt and ground black pepper
1/2 cup gluten free flour
8 tablespoons olive oil
1 small shallot, minced
1 cup low sodium chicken broth or stock
2 tablespoons small capers, rinsed and drained
3 tablespoons unsalted butter, softened
2 tablespoons minced fresh parsley leaves

Adjust an oven rack to the lower middle position, set a large baking dish or heat-proof serving plate on the rack, and heat the oven to 200°.

Sprinkle both sides of the chicken cutlets generously with salt and pepper. Measure the flour into a shallow baking dish or pie plate. Coat each chicken cutlet with flour and shake to remove excess.

Heat 4 tablespoons of the oil in a heavy bottomed 12 inch skillet over medium-high heat. Place half of the chicken cutlets in the skillet. Sauté until lightly browned, about 2 minutes on each side.

Remove the pan from the heat and transfer the cutlets to the plate in the oven. Repeat process with the remaining 4 tablespoons of oil and remaining chicken cutlets. Keep all cutlets warm in oven.

Add the shallot to the empty skillet. Sauté over medium heat until fragrant; about 30 seconds. Add the broth and lemon slices, increase the heat to high and scrape the bottom of the pan with a wooden spoon or spatula to loosen the browned bits. Simmer until the liquid reduces to 1/3 cup; about 4 minutes.

Add the lemon juice and capers and simmer until the sauce reduces again to 1/3 cup; about 1 minute. Remove the pan from the heat and stir in the butter until it melts and thickens the sauce. Stir in the parsley and season with salt and pepper to taste. Spoon the sauce over the chicken and serve immediately.

Serve with:
Steamed Asparagus with butter
Category A items of your choice
Category C items of your choice

Chili   **Category: C**   **Serves: 6-8**

1 tablespoon olive oil
1 lb. lean ground beef or ground turkey
1 medium green pepper, chopped
1 medium onion, chopped
1 stalk celery, chopped
3 cloves garlic, minced
1-8 oz. can tomato sauce
1-15 oz. can diced tomatoes
1 1/2 cups water
1-15 oz. can kidney beans <u>with</u> liquid
1-15 oz. can black beans, drained and rinsed
1 tablespoon chili powder
3 heaping teaspoons cumin
1/4 teaspoon cayenne pepper
1/2 teaspoon salt
1/4 teaspoon pepper

Grated Parmesan cheese for garnish (optional)
Sour cream for garnish (optional)

In a large skillet or Dutch oven over medium-high heat, sauté the ground beef, green pepper, onion, celery and garlic in the oil, breaking up the meat as it cooks.

Stir in the remaining ingredients except garnishes. Bring the contents to a boil and then reduce the heat. Cover the pan and simmer stirring occasionally for 15-20 minutes, until it thickens.

Serve with Parmesan cheese or sour cream, if desired

<u>Serve with:</u>
Category A items of your choice

Chachouka   **Category: B**   **Serves: 4-6**

1/4 cup extra virgin olive oil
3 cloves garlic, peeled
2 white onions, thinly sliced
1 each: green, red, and yellow peppers, seeded and cut into thick strips
1 red chili pepper, seeds removed, finely chopped
1-15 oz. can Great Northern beans, rinsed and drained
1-15 oz. can Chick peas, rinsed and drained
2-15 oz. cans diced tomatoes
Salt and ground black pepper to taste

Heat olive oil over medium heat in a large sauté pan or similar dish. Add garlic and fry until it begins to brown, then add onions and soften for 5-7 minutes. Add peppers and cook for 8-10 minutes, or until softened. Add tomatoes, beans, and chick peas.

Season with salt and pepper. Simmer, partially covered, for 10-15 minutes or until the mixture is softened.

Serve with:
Deviled Eggs
Cheese Bread
Category A items of your choice
Category B items of your choice

Parmesan Crusted Chicken Category: C Serves: 4

Four boneless skinless chicken breast halves
8 teaspoons sherry
1/3 teaspoon plus 1/4 teaspoon ground black pepper
2 cups coarsely shredded Parmesan cheese (do <u>not</u> use canned grated cheese)
1/3 cup gluten free bread crumbs
1 tablespoon plus 3 tablespoons olive oil
1 medium onion, chopped
1 small green pepper, chopped
1 teaspoon minced garlic
1 teaspoon basil
1 teaspoon oregano
1/4 teaspoon salt
4 plum Roma tomatoes, chopped
2 tablespoons minced fresh parsley

Combine 1/3 teaspoon of pepper, the cheese and bread crumbs together on a sheet of wax paper.

Pour sherry into a shallow bowl. Dip each chicken breast in sherry, moisten both sides, and then press the breasts firmly into the cheese mixture covering both sides of the breast.

In a medium skillet over medium heat, sauté the onion, green pepper, and garlic in 1 tablespoon of olive oil, stirring frequently until the vegetables are tender. Stir in the basil, oregano, salt, 1/4 teaspoon of pepper, tomatoes and parsley. Continue cooking until the mixture is heated through.

Preheat a large non-stick skillet over medium heat. Add 3 tablespoons of olive oil or more if needed to coat bottom of skillet. Set the breasts in the skillet and cook 5-6 minutes on each side (turning carefully with a wide spatula), until the cheese is lightly golden and the chicken is cooked through.

Remove the breasts from the skillet and set on paper towels to remove excess oil. Serve the chicken with the tomato mixture spooned over them.

Serve with:

Caprese Salad

Tossed Salad

Category A items of your choice

Category C items of your choice

Pork Chops with Caramelized Onions   **Category: C**   **Serves: 4**

Four 3/4 inch thick pork chops
1/2 cup Marsala wine
Nonstick cooking spray
1/4 teaspoon salt
1/8 teaspoon pepper
8 slices bacon
1 large white onion, sliced thinly
8 oz. fresh sliced mushrooms
1 teaspoon brown sugar
1/3 cup hot water
1 gluten free chicken bouillon cube

Place the pork chops and wine in a gallon sized self seal bag (zip lock) and marinate the meat for at least 2 hours in the refrigerator.

Preheat the broiler, and spray an 8 x 11 inch baking dish with cooking spray. Remove the pork chops from the marinade and sprinkle them with salt and pepper. Set them in the prepared baking dish.

In a large skillet, cook the bacon, drain it on paper towels, and then crumble it. Reserve 2 tablespoons of the bacon drippings.

In the same skillet, add the onions and mushrooms and the reserved drippings and cook over medium heat, stirring occasionally, until the onions begin to soften. Stir the brown sugar into the skillet and cook for 5 minutes longer, or until the onions and mushrooms are completely browned.

In a small bowl, stir together the water and bouillon until the cube has dissolved. Add to the onion mixture and boil until the liquid is reduced by half, scraping up any brown bits from the bottom of the skillet. Stir in the bacon crumbles.

Broil the pork chops for about 5 minutes on each side; or just until the meat is cooked through and the internal temperature is 160°.

Spoon the onion-mushroom mixture over the pork chops and serve.

<u>Serve with:</u>
Sherry's Delicious Cabbage
Category A items of your choice
Category C items of your choice

Crab Cakes with Creamy   **Category: C**   **Serves: 2-4**
Chipotle Sauce

1 lb. jumbo lump crab meat, picked over to remove shells
4 scallions, green parts only, minced (about 1/2 cup)
1 tablespoon chopped fresh herbs; choose from: cilantro, dill, basil, or parsley leaves
1 1/2 teaspoons Old Bay seasoning
2-4 tablespoons plain dry gluten free bread crumbs
1/4 cup mayonnaise
Salt and ground white pepper
1 large egg, beaten
1/4 cup gluten free flour
1/4 cup olive oil

Gently fold the crab meat, scallions, herbs, Old Bay, 2 tablespoons bread crumbs, and mayonnaise together in a medium bowl, being careful not to break the lumps of crab. Season with salt and white pepper to taste. Carefully fold in the egg with rubber spatula until the mixture just clings together. Add more crumbs if mixture is too moist and loose.

Divide the crab mixture into four portions and shape each into a fat, round cake, about 3 inches across and 1 1/2 inches high. Arrange on a baking sheet lined with wax or parchment paper; cover with plastic wrap and chill for at least 30 minutes. (They may be refrigerated for up to 24 hours prior to cooking.)

Put the flour on a plate or in a pie tin. Lightly dredge the crab cakes in the flour. Heat the oil in a large skillet over moderate-high heat until hot but not smoking. Gently lay the chilled crab cakes in the skillet and pan fry until the outsides are crisp and browned; 4-5 minutes per side. Serve immediately with Chipotle sauce.

For the sauce:
1/4 cup mayonnaise
1/4 cup sour cream
2 teaspoons minced gluten free chipotle chilies in adobo sauce *
1 small garlic clove, minced or pressed
2 teaspoons minced fresh cilantro leaves
1 teaspoon of lime juice (preferably fresh)

Mix all ingredients together in a small bowl. Cover and refrigerate until the flavors blend; about 30 minutes. The sauce can be refrigerated for several days.

*Available at Hispanic markets, some specialty food shops, and some supermarkets

Serve with:
Tossed Salad
Category A items of your choice
Category C items of your choice

Chicken Vermouth   **Category: C**   **Serves: 4**

4 whole boneless, skinless chicken breasts
1/4 cup gluten free flour
2 tablespoons olive oil
3 cloves garlic, peeled and minced
1/2 cup dry vermouth
8 fresh mushrooms, thinly sliced
Juice from 1 lemon
2 tablespoons butter
1 tablespoon gluten free Worcestershire sauce
2 tablespoons Dijon mustard
Salt and black pepper to taste
4 sprigs Italian parsley, chopped

Thoroughly trim the chicken breasts, separate into halves. Place them between two sheets of plastic wrap and pound to about 1/2 inch thickness. Coat them with flour on all sides.

In a large sauce pan, heat the olive oil over medium-high heat. Add the chicken and sauté until lightly browned, about 2 minutes each side (or until done). Remove the chicken and set aside, covered with foil to keep warm.

Drain the excess oil, reserving just enough to coat the bottom of the pan. Place the pan over medium-high heat; add garlic and sauté for 2 minutes or until soft and fragrant. Add the dry vermouth, butter, mushrooms, lemon juice, Dijon mustard, Worcestershire sauce, and parsley. Sauté for 3 minutes; stirring to combine. Season with salt and pepper and remove from heat.

Serve the sauce over the chicken.

Serve with:
Steamed Broccoli or Spinach with olive oil and salt
Category A items of your choice
Category C items of your choice

Sea Bass   **Category: C**   **Serves: 4**

4 sea bass fillets, 8-10 oz. each
1/4 cup gluten free flour
1 teaspoon salt
1 teaspoon ground black pepper
1 teaspoon garlic powder
1/2 cup olive oil
4 cloves garlic, peeled and sliced thin
4 artichoke hearts, canned in water, halved and patted dry
1/4 cup sundried tomatoes in oil, chopped
1/4 cup capers, drained
1 tablespoon fresh lemon juice
4 tablespoons butter
1 tablespoon fresh parsley, minced
1/4 cup white wine or chicken broth or stock

Preheat the oven to 400°.

In a bowl, mix the flour, salt, pepper and garlic powder. Dust the sea bass on both sides with the flour mixture.

Coat the bottom of a large skillet with the oil and heat over medium-high heat. Add the sea bass and sauté for 2-3 minutes. Turn and sauté the other side for 2-3 minutes until golden brown. Transfer the sea bass to a baking dish and bake for 5-10 minutes, or until done to your preference.

Add the sliced garlic to the skillet and sauté about 1 minute. Add the artichokes, sundried tomatoes, and capers. Sauté for 1 minute, then add the lemon juice. Add the wine or chicken stock and simmer 5 minutes or until wine is reduced by half. Add the butter and parsley, and stir to combine. Serve sea bass with sauce.

Serve with:
Spring Greens with Beets & Goat Cheese
Category A items of your choice
Category C items of your choice

Gluten Free Pizza Crust   **Category: B**   **Makes: 1 12-inch crust**

3/4 cup brown rice flour
1/3 cup potato starch
1 teaspoon granulated sugar
1 1/2 teaspoon Xanthan gum
1 1/2 teaspoon bread machine or instant yeast
1/2 teaspoon salt
1 teaspoon dried oregano leaves
3/4 cup water
1 teaspoon apple cider vinegar
1 tablespoon vegetable oil
2 to 3 tablespoons sweet rice flour

Mixer Method

In a large bowl or plastic bag, combine brown rice flour, potato starch, sugar, Xanthan gum, yeast, salt and oregano. Mix well and set aside.

In a separate bowl, using a heavy-duty electric mixer with paddle attachment, combine water, vinegar and oil until well blended.

With the mixer on the lowest speed, slowly add the dry ingredients until combined. With a rubber spatula, scrape the bottom and sides of the bowl. With the mixer on medium speed, beat for 4 minutes.

Bread Machine Method

In a large bowl or plastic bag, combine brown rice flour, potato starch, sugar, Xanthan gum, yeast, salt and oregano. Mix well and set aside.

Pour water, vinegar and oil into the bread machine baking pan. Select the Dough Cycle. Allow the liquids to mix until combined.

Gradually add the dry ingredients as the bread machine is mixing, scraping with a rubber spatula while adding. Try to incorporate all the dry ingredients within 1 to 2 minutes. Allow the bread machine to complete the cycle.

To Prepare Pizza

With a wet rubber spatula, remove the (very sticky) dough to generously greased pizza pan or large cookie sheet, spreading out as much as possible. Generously sprinkle with sweet rice flour. With floured fingers, gently pat out dough to fill the pan evenly. Continue to sprinkle with sweet rice flour as required. Form a rim at the edge of pan.

Allow to rise in a warm, draft-free place for 15 minutes. Bake at 400° for 12 to 15 minutes or until firm. Spread with your choice of toppings (see recipes on pages 145 and 146).

Return to oven and finish baking according to topping recipe directions.

Roasted Vegetable Pizza Topping   **Category: B**   **Makes: Topping for 1 Pizza**

1/2 cup extra virgin olive oil
1 small Italian eggplant cut into 1/2 inch cubes
1 large red bell pepper, cut into 1/2 inch slices
1 large yellow bell pepper, cut into 1/2 inch slices
2 cups Portobello mushrooms, cut into 1/2 inch slices
4 small zucchini, cut into 1/2 inch slices
5 cloves garlic, minced
3/4 cup shredded Mozzarella cheese
1/3 cup freshly grated Parmesan cheese
1 partially baked pizza crust (see page 143)

Preheat oven to 425°.

Measure oil into large roasting pan. Add vegetables and garlic. Toss to coat. Roast in preheated oven, turning once, for 10-15 minutes or until tender. Do not overcook. Set aside to cool.

To assemble, sprinkle half the Mozzarella cheese over the partially baked pizza crust. Top with roasted vegetables, remaining Mozzarella and Parmesan.

Reduce heat to 400° and bake for 12-15 minutes or until the topping is bubbly and cheese is melted, lightly browned and heated through. Serve immediately.

Serve with:
Tossed Salad
Category A items of your choice
Category B items of your choice

Five-Cheese Pizza Topping   **Category: C**   **Makes: Topping for 1 Pizza**

1 to 2 oz. shredded sharp or medium Cheddar cheese
1 to 2 oz. Mozzarella cheese
1 to 2 oz. Havarti cheese
1 to 2 oz. grated Asiago cheese
1 to 2 oz. Fontina Cheese
1 1/2 cups *Fresh Salsa* (see page 63) or prepared salsa
1 partially baked pizza crust (see page 143)

Preheat oven to 400°.

In a small bowl, mix together cheeses. Set aside.

Spread salsa over pizza crust, then top with cheese mixture.

Bake in preheated oven for 15-20 minutes or until cheese is lightly browned and heated through.

Serve with:
Tossed Salad
Category A items of your choice
Category B items of your choice

Chicken with Rosemary Butter Sauce   Category: C   Serves: 4

4 boneless skinless chicken breast halves (4 oz. each)
5 tablespoons butter, divided
1/2 cup white wine or chicken broth
1/2 cup heavy cream
1 tablespoon minced fresh rosemary

In a large skillet over medium heat, cook the chicken in 2 tablespoons butter for 4-5 minutes on each side or until juices run clear. Remove and keep warm.

Add wine to pan; cook over medium-low heat, stirring to loosen browned bits from pan. Add cream and bring to a boil. Reduce heat; cook and stir until slightly thickened.

Stir in rosemary and remaining butter until blended.

Serve sauce with chicken.

Serve with:
Arugula Salad with Garlic Balsamic Vinaigrette
Category A items of your choice
Category C items of your choice

Mahi-mahi with Tomato, Caper　　　　**Category: C**　　　　　　　**Serves: 4**
and Olive Tapenade

For the fish:
4 Mahi-mahi fillets (6 oz. each) or other firm whitefish of your choice
1/4 cup olive oil
Salt, ground black pepper and garlic powder for seasoning

For the sauce:
2 tablespoons extra virgin olive oil
2 teaspoons minced garlic
2 cups diced canned tomatoes, drained (or fresh if good ones are available)
½ cup pitted chipped brine-cured black olives (such as Kalamata)
2 tablespoons capers, drained
Freshly ground black pepper

Prepare fish: Heat oil in a large skillet over medium-high heat. Generously season fish fillets with salt, pepper and garlic powder.

Cook fish, turning once until just done (about 8 minutes total per inch of thickness). Do not overcook. Remove fish from skillet, place on a platter, cover and keep warm.

Prepare sauce: Heat the olive oil in a small, heavy saucepan over medium heat. Add the garlic and cook for 1 minute. Add the tomatoes, olives, and capers. Bring to a simmer and reduce the heat. Cook uncovered, for about 5 minutes, until the tomatoes have wilted. Season with pepper to taste.

Serve with roasted or grilled fish fillets.

Serve with:
Mixed Green Salad with *Coci Helen's Salad Dressing* or other gluten free dressing of your choice
Steamed green beans with butter
Category A items of your choice
Category C items of your choice

Roasted Leg of Lamb with Garlic   **Category: C**   **Serves: 6-8**

1 (5-6 lb.) leg of lamb (allow 1 lb. per person of uncooked trimmed leg of lamb)
Olive oil
1/4 cup sliced garlic
Dried rosemary
Salt and freshly ground black pepper

Preheat the oven to 425°. Place the rack in the center of the oven.

Place the lamb on a roasting rack in a shallow roasting pan. Trim the excess fat and make 10 to 12 long, shallow slits in the meat. Rub the entire leg with olive oil. Push garlic slices gently into the slits. Sprinkle the meat liberally with the rosemary, salt, and pepper. Allow the lamb to come to room temperature.

Place the pan on the oven rack just below the center of the oven and roast for 15 minutes; turn the oven heat down to 350°. Roast for another hour, until the internal temperature registers 150° for medium rare, or 155° for medium.

Allow to rest for 15 minutes before carving.

<u>Serve with:</u>
Spinach Salad with Beets & Feta Cheese
Roasted Asparagus
Category A items of your choice
Category C items of your choice

Sautéed Sea Scallops with Creamy   Category: C   Serves: 2
Shallot Wine Sauce

1 lb. sea scallops, rinsed and patted dry
Salt and ground black pepper
4 tablespoons butter or Earth Balance
1/4 cup white wine
4 tablespoons bottled clam juice
2 tablespoons minced shallots
4 tablespoons heavy cream

Season the scallops with salt and pepper, to taste. Heat the butter in a large, heavy skillet over high heat. Add the scallops and cook for 1 1/2 minutes, until just firm and golden in color. Turn and cook the other side another 1 1/2 minutes. Transfer scallops to a small bowl and cover with foil.

Add the wine, clam juice, and shallots to the skillet; scrape up the pan drippings. Boil until the liquid is reduced to a little less than 1/4 cup. Stir in the heavy cream and add the scallops and any juices on the plate. Reduce the heat and cook another minute until the scallops and sauce are heated through. Serve immediately.

Serve with:
Tossed Salad
Sautéed Zucchini topped with Parmesan or Romano cheese
Category A items of your choice
Category C items of your choice

Rigatoni with Eggplant in   **Category: B**   **Serves: 6**
Cream Curry Sauce

1 1-lb. eggplant, diced
1/2 cup extra-virgin olive oil
3/4 lb. zucchini, diced
1 medium onion, diced
2 cups tomato purée (not paste)
Salt and ground black pepper to taste
1 1/2 cups heavy cream or half and half
1 tablespoon curry powder
1 lb. gluten free rigatoni
1 cup fresh finely chopped basil
1/2 cup freshly grated Parmesan cheese

Sprinkle salt over the eggplant and drain in a colander for about 1 hour. Dry the eggplant with kitchen towels. Heat 1/4 cup of the oil in a large skillet over medium heat, add the eggplant and sauté until tender. Remove, drain on paper towels and set aside.

Sauté the zucchini in the remaining oil until crisp-tender. Remove, drain on paper towels and set aside.

Sauté the onion in the same skillet until transparent, 6-8 minutes. Add the tomato puree and salt and pepper to taste. Cover and cook for 8 minutes over medium heat. Remove from the heat and stir in the cream and curry powder.

Boil the rigatoni until al dente, drain and add it to the skillet. Add the eggplant, zucchini, and the basil. Mix well over high heat for several minutes to bring the sauce and pasta together. Serve immediately with Parmesan on the side.

Serve with:
Mixed Green Salad
Sourdough Bread
Category A items of your choice
Category B items of your choice

Salmon Steaks with Balsamic Mustard Glaze   Category: C   Serves: 4

4 skin-on salmon steaks (about 6 oz. each)
1/4 teaspoon salt
1/4 teaspoon ground black pepper
1 teaspoon Dijon mustard
2 tablespoons olive oil
1 tablespoon Balsamic vinegar
1/2 teaspoon dried dill weed or dried herb of your choice
Fresh lemon wedges

Sprinkle the salmon with the salt and pepper. In a cup, whisk together the mustard, oil, Balsamic vinegar, and dill. Brush a thick layer of the glaze on each salmon steak and let stand 15 minutes at room temperature.

Preheat grill or oven broiler. Cook the steaks to the desired degree of doneness, turning once (about 8 minutes per inch of thickness). Do not overcook.

Serve salmon immediately with fresh lemon wedges.

Serve with:
Baby Carrots with Maple Butter
Sautéed Spinach with olive oil or butter
Category A items of your choice
Category C items of your choice

Pasta Primavera   **Category: B**   **Serves: 4**

6 tablespoons olive oil, divided
1 1/2 cups plum tomatoes, chopped
2 cloves garlic, minced and divided
Dash salt
2 cups porcini or button mushrooms, roughly chopped
Dash ground black pepper
2 cups asparagus tips (blanched in boiling, salted water for 1 minute)
1 medium zucchini (quartered, cut into 1-inch lengths, and blanched in boiling water for 2 minutes)
1/2 cup frozen peas, thawed
1 cup heavy cream
2/3 cup Parmigiano-Reggiano, plus additional for garnish
2 tablespoons butter or Earth Balance
1 lb. gluten free spaghetti
1/2 cup pine nuts (lightly toasted)
2 tablespoons fresh basil, cut into thin strips

Heat 2 tablespoons of the olive oil in a medium sauté pan over high heat. Add tomatoes, half of the garlic, and a pinch of salt and cook, stirring or tossing occasionally, about 4-8 minutes. Set aside and keep warm.

Heat 2 tablespoons of the olive oil in a medium sauté pan over high heat and sauté the mushrooms with half of the remaining garlic and pinch of salt until they've given off most their water and are browned, about 8-10 minutes. Set aside, season to taste with salt and pepper and keep warm.

Heat the remaining 2 tablespoons of olive oil over medium high heat in a large sauté pan, add remaining garlic, and cook the blanched vegetables until they've taken on a little color but are still firm, about 3-5 minutes. Set aside, season to taste, and keep warm.

Bring a large pot of salted water to boil. Meanwhile, simmer cream until reduced by half in a small sauce pan, stir in the Parmesan and butter, cover and remove from heat. Cook the spaghetti, drain and return to pot. Add cream mixture and toss.

Transfer the spaghetti and cream to a bowl large enough to hold all the ingredients and bring it to the table, with the reserved tomato sauce, mushrooms, sautéed vegetables, peas and the pine nuts each in separate bowls.

Toss the spaghetti first with the mushrooms, then the sautéed vegetables and peas, then portion it into warmed pasta plates. Garnish each plate with toasted pine nuts, tomato sauce, a pinch of basil, and freshly grated Parmesan, with salt and pepper to taste.

Serve with:
Tossed Salad
Herbed Italian Bread
Category A items of your choice
Category B items of your choice

Spinach-Stuffed Portobellos   **Category: A**   **Serves: 4**

4 large Portobello mushrooms
2 tablespoons olive oil
1-14.5 oz. can diced tomatoes, drained
1-10 oz. package frozen chopped spinach, thawed and squeezed dry
3 tablespoons chopped green onions
2 tablespoons grated Romano cheese
1/4 teaspoon crushed red pepper flakes
1/8 teaspoon salt
1/2 cup shredded part-skim Mozzarella cheese

Remove and discard stems and gills from mushrooms. In a large skillet over medium heat, cook mushrooms in oil for 10-15 minutes or just until tender, turning once.

In a small bowl, combine the tomatoes, spinach, onions, Romano cheese, pepper flakes and salt. Spoon into mushroom caps. Sprinkle with Mozzarella cheese.

Place on a baking sheet lined with heavy-duty foil.

Bake at 375° for 10-15 minutes or until heated through and cheese is melted.

Serve with:
Roasted Garlic Bread
Mixed Green Salad
Category A items of your choice

Grilled Snapper with Caper Sauce   **Category: C**   **Serves: 4**

1/4 cup fresh lime juice
1 jalapeno pepper, seeded
3 garlic cloves, peeled
1 1/4 teaspoons fresh thyme leaves or 1/4 teaspoon dried thyme
1 teaspoon salt
1 teaspoon ground black pepper
4 red snapper fillets (6 oz. each)

Sauce:
1 tablespoon lime juice
1/4 cup olive oil
2 tablespoons water
1 teaspoon red wine vinegar
1/2 cup fresh cilantro leaves
1 shallot, peeled
1 tablespoon capers, drained
1 1/2 teaspoons chopped seeded jalapeno pepper
1 clove garlic, peeled and halved
1/4 teaspoon pepper

Prepare marinade: In a small food processor, combine the first six ingredients; cover and process until blended. Pour into a large resealable plastic bag. Add the fish fillets; seal the bag and turn to coat. Refrigerate for 30 minutes.

Meanwhile, combine sauce ingredients in a small food processor. Cover and process until blended.

Coat grill rack or oven broiling pan with cooking spray; preheat grill or oven broiler.

Remove fish from bag; drain and discard marinade. Grill or broil fillets turning once until fish flakes easily with a fork (about 8 minutes total per inch of thickness).

Serve fish with sauce.

Serve with:
Mixed Green Salad
Sautéed Green Beans with Butter
Category A items of your choice
Category C items of your choice

Barbecue Baked Beans and Sausage   Category: C   Serves: 4

1/2 cup prepared gluten free barbecue sauce
1/2 cup water
2 tablespoons tomato paste
1 tablespoon molasses
Salt and ground black pepper to taste
1 tablespoon olive oil
1 medium onion, chopped
4 cups chopped collard greens (about 10 oz.), tough stems removed
9 oz. cooked turkey Italian sausage links (about 3), halved lengthwise and sliced
2 cans Great Northern or Navy beans, drained and rinsed

Whisk barbecue sauce, water, tomato paste, molasses, salt, and pepper in a medium bowl.

Heat oil in a large saucepan over medium heat. Add onion and collard greens and cook, stirring occasionally, until the collards are wilted, 3-5 minutes. Add sausage and cook, stirring, until beginning to brown, about 3 minutes more.

Reduce heat to medium-low; add beans and the sauce mixture to the pan. Gently stir to combine, cover and cook until heated through, about 3 minutes.

Serve with:
Tossed Salad
Category A items of your choice
Category C items of your choice

Black Bean Tostados with　　　　　**Category: B**　　　　　**Serves: 6-8**
Roasted Tomatillo Sauce

6 large garlic cloves, 4 cloves peeled and left whole and 2 cloves coarsely chopped
1 lb. tomatillos (8 medium), rinsed and halved (available at Hispanic markets and many supermarkets)
4 fresh Serrano chilies or 2 fresh jalapenos (including seeds), coarsely chopped
3/4 cup coarsely chopped fresh cilantro sprigs
2 cups plus 2 to 3 tablespoons water
1/2 cup finely chopped white onion
1 3/4 teaspoons salt
2-15 oz. can black beans, rinsed and drained
3 tablespoons olive oil
2 firm, ripe avocados
12 gluten free corn tostados
3 cups thinly sliced romaine
2 cups crumbled queso fresco (Mexican fresh cheese) or grated sharp Cheddar cheese

Make tomatillo sauce:

Line a 10-inch heavy skillet (preferably cast-iron; not nonstick) with foil, then heat over moderately high heat until hot but not smoking. Add 2 whole garlic cloves and half of the tomatillos, cut sides down, and roast on top of stove until well browned, 4 to 5 minutes (skillet will begin to smoke at this point).

Turn over garlic and tomatillos (tomatillos may stick to foil) and roast until well browned and tomatillos are completely soft, 3-4 minutes. Transfer roasted garlic and tomatillos to a food processor. Discard foil, then line skillet with a fresh sheet of foil and roast remaining 2 whole garlic cloves and remaining tomatillos in same manner, transferring when done to food processor. Cool garlic and tomatillos to room temperature in bowl of processor, about 30 minutes.

Add chilies, half of cilantro, and 2 tablespoons water to mixture in processor, then pulse until it forms a chunky sauce, adding 1 tablespoon more water if too thick. Transfer to a bowl and stir in onion and 1 teaspoon salt.

Bring beans and remaining 2 cups water to a simmer in a 3-quart heavy saucepan, stirring occasionally. Drain beans, reserving liquid. Purée beans, 1/4 cup cooking liquid (reserve remainder), avocado and chopped garlic in a food processor until smooth.

Heat oil in a 10-inch heavy skillet over moderate heat until hot but not smoking, then add bean purée and cook, stirring, until very thick, about 5 minutes. Stir in remaining 3/4 teaspoon salt, then remove from heat and keep warm, covered.

If necessary, stir some of reserved bean-cooking liquid in to make bean purée soft and easily spreadable. Divide warm bean puree among tostadas and spread evenly. Spoon 1 tablespoon tomatillo sauce over each tostada, then divide avocado among tostadas and top with romaine, cheese, and remaining cilantro.

Serve remaining tomatillo sauce on the side.

Serve with:
Sour cream
Sliced gluten free black olives
Category A items of your choice
Category B items of your choice

Turkey Chipotle Chili   **Category: C**   **Serves: 6-8**

2 canned whole gluten free chipotle chilies in adobo sauce* or 2 dried whole chipotle chilies*
1 cup hot water, boiling if using the dried chilies
2 lbs. fresh tomatillos * or 3-18 oz. cans whole tomatillos*, drained
2 large onions, chopped
8 garlic cloves, minced
1/4 cup olive oil
2 heaping tablespoons ground cumin
2 lbs. ground turkey
2 cups chicken broth or stock
1 bay leaf
1 1/2 teaspoons dried oregano, crumbled
2 teaspoons salt, or to taste
1 green bell pepper, chopped
2-4 oz. cans mild green chilies, drained and chopped
1 tablespoon cornmeal
3-15 oz. cans white beans, rinsed and drained
1/2 cup chopped fresh cilantro
Sour cream as an accompaniment if desired

*available at Hispanic markets, some specialty food shops, and some supermarkets

If using the canned chipotle chilies, purée them in a blender with the hot water and set aside. If using dried chipotle chilies, stem and seed them (being sure to thoroughly wash hands afterward); place in a small bowl. Add boiling water, let them soak for 20 minutes, then place in blender, purée and set aside.

Place the fresh or canned, drained tomatillos in a blender; puree and set aside.

In a large, heavy kettle, Dutch oven or soup pot, cook the onions and 5 of the garlic cloves in the oil over moderate heat, stirring, until the onions are softened. Add the cumin and cook the mixture, stirring, for 30 seconds.

Add the turkey and cook the mixture, stirring and breaking up the lumps, until the turkey is no longer pink. Add the chipotle purée, the tomatillo purée, the broth, the bay leaf, the orégano, and the salt and simmer the mixture, uncovered, adding more water if necessary to keep the turkey barely covered, for 1 hour.

Stir in the bell pepper, the canned green chilies and the cornmeal and simmer the mixture, stirring occasionally, for 30 minutes. Stir in the white beans, the cilantro, the remaining 2 garlic cloves, minced, and salt to taste.

Simmer the chili for 3-5 minutes, or until the beans are heated through. Discard the bay leaf.

Serve with the sour cream.

Serve with:
Tossed Salad
Category A items of your choice
Category C items of your choice

Roast Beef with Mustard Caper Sauce   Category: C   Serves: 6

Roast Beef:
1 3-lb. eye of round beef roast
1/2 teaspoon salt
1 1/2 teaspoons dried thyme
1 1/2 teaspoons dried basil
1/2 teaspoon oregano
1/2 teaspoon freshly ground pepper
Olive oil for cooking

Sauce:
1 tablespoon butter or Earth Balance
1 tablespoon gluten free flour
2 cups beef broth or stock
2 tablespoons Dijon mustard
2 tablespoons drained capers
Salt and pepper to taste

Sprinkle beef with salt.

Preheat oven to 350°F. Mix thyme, basil, oregano and 1/2 teaspoon pepper in small bowl. Coat the bottom of an oven-proof skillet (preferably cast iron) with olive oil and heat over medium-high heat. Add beef and cook on all sides, turning occasionally, about 10 minutes or until browned. Sprinkle with herb mixture.

Transfer skillet to oven. Roast until meat thermometer inserted into center of meat registers 130°F, about 40 minutes, or to desired doneness. Transfer to cutting board; let rest.

Place skillet with beef juices over medium-high heat. Add butter; stir until melted. Whisk in gluten-free flour until smooth. Gradually whisk in beef broth. Bring to boil, reduce heat and simmer until sauce is reduced to 1 1/4 cups, whisking often, about 6-8 minutes. Whisk in mustard and capers. Season to taste with salt and pepper.

Cut beef crosswise into thin slices and serve with sauce.

Serve with:
Cauliflower Mashed "Potatoes"
Italian Broccoli Rabe
Roasted Asparagus
Category A items of your choice
Category C items of your choice

Sides

Cauliflower Mashed "Potatoes"   **Category: A**   **Serves: 6-8**

1 large head cauliflower, broken into florets
Salt and ground black pepper to taste
1/2 cup milk or cream
1 heaping tablespoon garlic, minced

In a large pan, boil cauliflower in salted water until tender. Drain all water and put cauliflower back into pan.

Mash cauliflower with a potato masher or electric mixer.

Add milk or cream and garlic and continue to mash until desired smoothness is achieved. Add additional milk or cream if desired.

Add salt and pepper to taste and serve.

Serve with:
Category A items of your choice
Category B OR Category C items of your choice

Indiana Succotash   **Category: A/B**   **Serves: 6**

6 ears corn, husked
Salt and ground black pepper
1 lb. green beans, trimmed and cut into 1/2 inch pieces
2 tablespoons unsalted butter
1 bunch scallions, cut into 1/4 inch pieces
1/2 teaspoon celery seeds
3/4 teaspoon paprika

Carefully slice kernels from corn using a sharp knife.

Bring a large pot of water to a boil, and season with 1 tablespoon salt. Cook beans until crisp-tender, about 3 minutes; remove using a wire-mesh skimmer, and spread out on a baking sheet or plate to cool.

Melt butter in a medium skillet over medium heat. Cook scallions and celery seeds until scallions begin to soften, about 5 minutes. Add corn and 1 teaspoon salt, cook until heated through, 3-5 minutes. Stir in beans and paprika. Season with salt and pepper, and cook until heated through, about 2 minutes.

Serve with:
Category A items of your choice
Category B items of your choice

Creamed Corn   **Category: B**   **Serves: 6**

9 ears fresh corn, husked
4 tablespoons unsalted butter
1 garlic clove, minced
1 teaspoon finely chopped fresh thyme
1 1/4 teaspoons coarse salt

Grate 6 ears of corn on the large holes of a box grater into a bowl. Carefully slice off kernels from remaining 3 cobs using a sharp knife; transfer to bowl. Scrape cobs with back of the blade to extract creamy liquid into bowl.

Melt 1 tablespoon butter in a medium saucepan over medium heat. Cook garlic until fragrant, about 30 seconds. Stir in corn with liquid, thyme and salt. Reduce heat to medium-low; cook, covered, stirring often, until corn is tender but still has a slight bite, 25-30 minutes.

Stir in remaining 3 tablespoons butter until melted. Serve immediately.

Serve with:
Category A items of your choice
Category B items of your choice

Calico Beans   **Category: B**   **Serves: 12**

4 medium onions, halved and sliced
5 bacon strips, diced
2 garlic cloves, minced
1 cup packed dark brown sugar
1/2 cup apple cider vinegar
1/4 teaspoon ground mustard
2-15 oz. cans lima beans, rinsed and drained
2-15 oz. cans pork and beans
1-16 oz. can kidney beans, rinsed and drained

In a Dutch oven, sauté the onions, bacon and garlic until onions are tender. Add brown sugar, vinegar and mustard; bring to a boil. Reduce heat; simmer, uncovered, for 20 minutes. Stir in beans.

Transfer to a 3-quart baking dish. Cover and bake at 350° for 1 hour or until heated through.

Serve with:
Category A items of your choice
Category B items of your choice

Risotto   **Category: B**   **Serves: 2-4**

1 cup Arborio rice
1/4 cup water
1 1/2 cups chicken or vegetable broth or stock
2 tablespoons butter
1/2 cup heavy cream
1/2 cup grated Parmesan cheese
1/2 teaspoon salt
1/2 teaspoon pepper

Combine rice, water and chicken broth in a medium saucepan. Bring to a boil. Cook over medium-high heat until most of the liquid is absorbed, stirring constantly.

Add butter, cover and simmer over low heat for five minutes. Stir in heavy cream and Parmesan cheese. Continue stirring over low heat until cheese is melted, approximately five minutes.

Add salt and pepper and serve immediately.

Serve with:
Category A items of your choice
Category B items of your choice

Dal (Curried Lentils)   **Category: B**   **Serves: 4**

1 tablespoon olive oil
1 cup minced onion
2 teaspoons minced garlic
1 tablespoon curry powder
1 teaspoon fresh grated ginger
1 fresh medium-sized jalapeno pepper, seeded and minced
4 cups low-sodium vegetable broth or stock
1 1/2 cups diced fresh tomatoes, or 1-14.5 oz. can diced tomatoes, including juice
1 cup dried lentils, washed
1 medium-sized sweet potato, peeled and diced
1 teaspoon salt
1/4 cup finely chopped fresh cilantro, for garnish
Salt and freshly ground black pepper

Heat the olive oil in a large, heavy (5 quart) saucepan over medium-high heat. Add the onion, garlic, curry powder, ginger, and jalapeno pepper and sauté for about 4 minutes.

Add the broth, tomatoes, lentils, sweet potato, and salt and bring to a boil. Reduce the heat to medium; cover loosely and simmer until the lentils are tender, about 30 minutes.

Just before serving, add the cilantro and season with the salt and pepper, to taste. Serve warm.

Serve with:
Category A items of your choice
Category B items of your choice

Black Beans with Corn and Tomato   Category: B   Serves: 4

1-15.5 oz. can black beans
1 cup frozen corn kernels, thawed
3 medium-sized plum tomatoes, seeded and cut into small pieces
4 medium-sized scallions, thinly sliced
1/4 cup chopped fresh cilantro
4 tablespoons olive oil
1 tablespoon red wine vinegar
2 heaping teaspoons ground cumin
Salt and ground black pepper to taste

Rinse the beans with water and drain well. Blot with a paper towel to remove as much moisture as possible. Place the beans in a medium-sized bowl and add the corn, tomatoes, scallions, and cilantro. Toss with the olive oil, red wine vinegar, and cumin. Season with salt and pepper to taste.

Serve at room temperature.

Serve with:
Category A items of your choice
Category B items of your choice

Garlicky Green Beans with Arugula   **Category: A**   **Serves: 4-6**

1 1/2 pounds green beans, trimmed
2 tablespoons extra-virgin olive oil
3 large garlic cloves, thinly sliced lengthwise
1/2 pound arugula, rinsed, stems discarded and leaves chopped (about 6 cups)
1/2 teaspoon finely grated fresh lemon zest
3/4 teaspoon salt
1/2 teaspoon ground black pepper

Cook beans in a pot of boiling salted water, uncovered, until tender, 4 to 6 minutes. Drain and set aside.

Heat oil in a 12-inch skillet over medium-high heat until hot but not smoking. Sauté garlic, stirring, until golden and fragrant, about 1 minute. Add beans, arugula, lemon zest, salt and pepper and cook, tossing, until arugula is wilted, about 2 minutes.

Can be served hot or at room temperature.

Serve with:
Category A items of your choice
Category B OR Category C items of your choice

Roasted Brussels Sprouts   **Category: A**   **Serves: 4-6**

1 1/2 pounds Brussels sprouts, ends trimmed, halved if medium-sized or quartered if large
1/2 cup extra-virgin olive oil
1 teaspoon salt
Dash ground black pepper

Preheat oven to 425°.

Place Brussels sprouts in a large baking dish, roasting pan or cast iron skillet. Drizzle with olive oil; sprinkle with salt and pepper.

Roast for 10 minutes; remove from oven and toss, adding a little more olive oil if sprouts appear dry.

Return to oven and continue roasting for 15 minutes or until browned and tender.

Serve with:
Category A items of your choice
Category B OR Category C items of your choice

Roasted Broccoli   **Category: A**   **Serves: 4-6**

2 large bunches broccoli, stalks peeled and sliced crosswise into 1/2 inch pieces, tops broken into florets
1/2 cup extra-virgin olive oil
1 teaspoon salt
Dash ground black pepper

Preheat oven to 425°.

Place broccoli in a large baking dish, roasting pan or cast iron skillet. Drizzle with olive oil; sprinkle with salt and pepper.

Roast for 5 minutes; remove from oven and toss, adding a little more olive oil if broccoli appears dry.

Return to oven and continue roasting for 5 minutes or until browned and tender.

Variation: Use cauliflower in place of broccoli, or a mixture of cauliflower and broccoli.

Serve with:
Category A items of your choice
Category B OR Category C items of your choice

Roasted Asparagus **Category: A** **Serves: 4-6**

2 1/2 pounds fresh asparagus spears, tough ends trimmed and discarded
1/2 cup extra-virgin olive oil
1 teaspoon salt
Dash ground black pepper

Preheat oven to 425°.

Place asparagus in a large baking dish, roasting pan or cast iron skillet. Drizzle with olive oil; sprinkle with salt and pepper.

Roast for 10 minutes; remove from oven and toss, adding a little more olive oil if asparagus appears dry.

Return to oven and continue roasting for 5-10 minutes or until tips are slightly browned and crisp and stalks are tender.

Note: Roasting time may vary and depends on thickness of asparagus spears.

Serve with:
Category A items of your choice
Category B OR Category C items of your choice

Italian Broccoli Rabe (Rapini)　　　　　**Category: A**　　　　　**Serves: 4-6**

2 pounds broccoli rabe
3/4 cup extra-virgin olive oil
5 cloves garlic, thinly sliced
Salt and ground black pepper to taste
Dash hot pepper flakes
Grated Romano cheese for garnish (optional)

Trim off lower portions of broccoli rabe stalks and discard; chop remaining portion of stalks, leaves and florets.

Heat 2 quarts salted water in a large saucepan until boiling. Add broccoli rabe and cook for 4-5 minutes or until crisp-tender. Drain, rinse with cool water, drain again and set aside.

Heat olive oil in a large skillet over medium-high heat. Add garlic and sauté until fragrant and slightly browned. Add broccoli rabe and cook and stir until heated through.

Remove from heat; add salt and pepper to taste and dash red pepper flakes. Stir to combine and serve immediately with grated Romano cheese if desired.

Serve with:
Category A items of your choice
Category B OR Category C items of your choice

Sherry's Delicious Cabbage   **Category: A**   **Serves: 4-6**

1 large head green cabbage, cored and shredded
1 large onion, chopped
2/3 cup butter or Earth Balance
1 1/2 teaspoons salt
1/2 teaspoon ground black pepper

Melt butter over medium heat in very large skillet (preferably cast iron if you have it). Add onion and sauté until golden, about 5-8 minutes.

Add cabbage and mix thoroughly. Continue cooking, tossing occasionally, until cabbage is tender and browned and onions are caramelized, adding more butter if necessary. Season with salt and pepper and serve.

Serve with:
Category A items of your choice
Category B OR Category C items of your choice

Baby Carrots with Maple Butter   **Category: B**   **Serves: 6-8**

2 pounds baby carrots
1/4 cup olive oil
1 teaspoon salt
2 tablespoons butter or Earth Balance, melted
2 tablespoons maple syrup

Preheat oven to 475º. Toss carrots with oil and salt; spread in a baking pan. Roast for 12 minutes.

While carrots are roasting, combine butter and maple syrup.

Remove carrots from oven, toss and drizzle with butter and maple syrup mixture and return to oven.
Roast for another 5-8 minutes or until browned and tender.

<u>Serve with:</u>
Category A items of your choice
Category B items of your choice

Yummy Fried Potatoes　　　　　　　**Category: B**　　　　　　　**Serves: 4-6**

6 large red or golden butter potatoes, unpeeled
1 large Vidalia onion, diced
1 red bell pepper, sliced
1 green bell pepper, sliced
8 oz. fresh mushrooms, sliced
1/2 cup butter or Earth Balance, divided
1/2 cup olive oil
1 tablespoon oregano
1 tablespoon chili powder
1 1/2 teaspoons salt or seasoned salt
1 teaspoon ground black pepper

If you have a large cast iron skillet, be sure to use it for this recipe! However, any large skillet will work just fine.

Scrub potatoes and cut into small chunks. Heat olive oil and 1/4 cup butter over medium heat in a very large skillet; add potatoes. Cook, flipping potatoes with a spatula occasionally for 15 minutes. Add onion and continue cooking for another 5 minutes. Add peppers and cook for another 8 minutes, continuing to flip potatoes, onions and peppers occasionally. (Add additional 1/4 cup butter if necessary to prevent sticking.)

Add mushrooms, oregano, chili powder, salt and pepper. Continue cooking as above until all vegetables are tender, potatoes are browned and crisp and onions are caramelized. Add additional salt and pepper to taste.

Serve with:
Category A items of your choice
Category B items of your choice

Snacks and Entertaining

Avocado Feta Salsa   **Category: A/C**   **Serves: 4-6**

1 large avocado, chopped
2 plum tomatoes, diced
1/4 cup red onion, chopped
1-3 cloves garlic (to taste), minced
1 teaspoon parsley, finely chopped
1/2 teaspoon oregano
1 tablespoon olive oil
1/2 tablespoon balsamic vinegar
4 oz. crumbled Feta cheese

Chop avocado and tomato in a large bowl. Add next 6 ingredients. Toss to coat, then fold in Feta cheese.

Serve with:
Sliced cucumbers, sliced radishes, celery sticks, carrot sticks, cauliflower florets
Gluten free tortilla chips or gluten free pita chips

Classic Margaritas   **Category: Beverage**   **Serves: 4**

4 lime slices
Coarse salt (optional)
2 cups ice cubes
1-6 oz. can (3/4 cup) frozen limeade, thawed
3/4 cup Tequila
1/4 cup Triple Sec. or other orange liqueur

Rub lime slices around rim of 4 glasses, and reserve lime slice. Dip rims of glasses into salt if desired.

Combine ice and next 3 ingredients in blender and blend until smooth.

Pour into glasses and garnish with lime slices.

Deviled Eggs   Category: C   Serves: 6-8

7 large eggs
3/4 teaspoon whole-grain mustard
3 tablespoons mayonnaise
1 1/2 teaspoons apple cider vinegar
1/4 teaspoon gluten free Worcestershire sauce
Salt and black pepper to taste

Place the eggs in a medium sauce pan and cover with 1 inch of water, and bring to a boil over high heat. Remove the pan from the heat, cover, and let it stand for 10 minutes. Meanwhile, fill a medium bowl with 1 quart of cold water and 14 ice cubes. Transfer the eggs to the ice water with a slotted spoon; let that sit for 5 minutes.

Peel the eggs and slice each in half, lengthwise with a paring knife. Remove the yolks to a small bowl. Arrange the whites on a serving dish. Mash the yolks with a fork until no large clumps remain. Add the mustard, mayonnaise, vinegar, Worcestershire, salt and pepper to taste; mix all of this with a rubber spatula, mashing the mixture against the side of the bowl until smooth.

Fit a pastry bag with a large open-star tip. Fill the bag with the yolk mixture, twisting the top of the pastry bag to help push the mixture toward the tip of the bag. Pipe the yolk mixture into the egg white halves, mounding the filling about 1/2 an inch above the flat surface of the whites. Chill or serve immediately.

Serve alone or with:
Chachouka

Guacamole   **Category: A/C**   **Serves: 6-8**

2 avocados
3 Roma tomatoes, seeded and chopped
1/2 medium red onion, chopped coarse
2 cloves garlic, chopped (3 cloves if you like more garlic)
6 sprigs fresh cilantro, chopped
Juice from 1/2 lemon or lime
2 teaspoons cumin, or more to taste
1/2 teaspoon red pepper, or more to taste
Salt and pepper to taste

Peel and mash avocados in a large bowl. Squeeze out 1/2 lemon or lime over avocados.

Add in tomatoes, onion, garlic, and cilantro. Stir together well.

Add all seasonings to mix, and adjust seasoning to taste. Stir and serve.

Serve with:
Sliced cucumbers, sliced radishes, celery sticks, carrot sticks, cauliflower florets
Gluten free tortilla chips or gluten free pita chips
Mexican dishes of your choice

Blue Cheese Balls   **Category: C**   **Makes: 2 4-inch Balls**

8 oz. cream cheese, softened
4 oz. blue cheese, crumbled
2 teaspoons prepared horseradish
3 to 4 drops hot pepper sauce
1 clove garlic, minced
3 green onions, finely chopped
1/2 cup chopped red, orange and/or yellow bell pepper
2 cups shredded Cheddar cheese
1 cup finely chopped pecans or almonds
1 Cherry or cherry tomato half (for the top-optional)

In a large bowl, combine cream cheese, blue cheese, horseradish, hot pepper sauce to taste and garlic. Set aside.

In a microwave-safe bowl, combine green onions and bell peppers. Microwave, covered, on High for 1 minute. (Or steam in a covered saucepan over low heat for 2-3 minutes or until tender-crisp).

Combine onion-pepper mixture with Cheddar cheese. Fold into cream cheese mixture. Divide in half and form into 2 balls. Wrap in plastic wrap and chill for 30-60 minutes. Roll in pecans or almonds. Garnish with cherry or cherry tomato on top.

Serve with:
Sliced cucumbers, sliced radishes, celery sticks, carrot sticks, cauliflower florets
Cheese Crackers, Cream Cheese Crackers or *Saltine Crackers*
Gluten free crackers of your choice

Parmesan Cheese Balls Category: C Makes: 2 4-inch Balls

2-8 oz. packages cream cheese, softened
1 cup grated Parmesan cheese
1/2 cup mayonnaise
1 teaspoon oregano
1 clove garlic, minced
1 cup finely chopped pecans or almonds
1 Cherry or cherry tomato half (for the top-optional)

Combine first 5 ingredients together. Divide in half and form 2 balls. Wrap in plastic wrap and chill for 30-60 minutes. Roll in pecans or almonds. Garnish with cherry or cherry tomato on top.

Serve with:
Sliced cucumbers, sliced radishes, celery sticks, carrot sticks, cauliflower florets
Cheese Crackers, Cream Cheese Crackers or *Saltine Crackers*
Gluten free crackers of your choice

Feta Spinach Dip　　　　　　　**Category: A/C**　　　　　　**Makes: 1 1/2 cups**

1-10 oz. package fresh spinach (about 5 cups)
3 oz. crumbled feta cheese
2 green onions, coarsely chopped
1/2 cup mayonnaise
1/2 cup plain yogurt
2 cloves minced fresh garlic
1 teaspoon oregano

In a microwave-safe bowl, microwave spinach, uncovered, on High for 2-3 minutes, stirring halfway through, until spinach is just wilted. Squeeze out excess moisture.

In a bowl, mix feta, green onions, mayonnaise and yogurt. Add garlic and oregano, then stir in spinach.

Refrigerate for at least 2 hours to allow flavors to develop and blend.

Serve with:
Sliced cucumbers, sliced radishes, celery sticks, carrot sticks, cauliflower florets
Cheese Crackers, Cream Cheese Crackers or *Saltine Crackers*
Gluten free crackers of your choice

Sundried Tomato Dip **Category: A/C** **Makes: 1 1/2 cups**

1/2 cup cream cheese, softened
1/2 cup plain yogurt
1/4 cup snipped sun-dried tomatoes
1/3 cup Asiago cheese
1/2 cup packed fresh cilantro, snipped

In a bowl, combine cream cheese and yogurt. Stir in sun-dried tomatoes, Asiago cheese and cilantro until combined.

Cover and refrigerate for at least 2 hours to allow flavors to develop and blend.

Serve with:
Sliced cucumbers, sliced radishes, celery sticks, carrot sticks, cauliflower florets
Cheese Crackers, Cream Cheese Crackers or *Saltine Crackers*
Gluten free crackers of your choice

Herb Vegetable Dip   **Category: A/C**   **Makes: 2 cups**

1 cup mayonnaise
1 cup sour cream
3 tablespoons grated onion
2 cloves garlic, minced
3 tablespoons chopped fresh dill or 3 teaspoons dried dill
Salt and ground black pepper to taste

Combine all ingredients in a food processor or blender until combined.

Refrigerate 3-4 hours before serving.

Serve with:
Sliced cucumbers, sliced radishes, celery sticks, carrot sticks, cauliflower florets
Cheese Crackers, Cream Cheese Crackers or *Saltine Crackers*
Gluten free crackers of your choice
Baked potatoes

Cucumber Dip   **Category: A/C**   **Makes 2 1/2 cups**

1 medium cucumber, finely chopped
1 clove garlic, minced
8 scallions, finely chopped
2 cups plain yogurt or sour cream
1/4 cup chopped fresh dill (or 1 tablespoon dried dill weed)
Salt and ground black pepper to taste

Mix cucumber, garlic, dill and scallions with yogurt or sour cream in a bowl. Add salt and pepper to taste. Refrigerate at least 2 hours.

Serve with:
Sliced cucumbers, sliced radishes, celery sticks, carrot sticks, cauliflower florets
Cheese Crackers, Cream Cheese Crackers or *Saltine Crackers*
Gluten free crackers of your choice

Roasted Red Pepper Dip   **Category: A/C**   **Makes: 1 1/2 cups**

1-7oz. jar roasted red peppers, drained
1 cup cream cheese
2 cloves garlic, minced
Salt ground black pepper to taste

Chop roasted red peppers and place in a food processor or blender until smooth. Add cream cheese, garlic, and salt and pepper to taste.

Refrigerate 2-3 hours before serving.

<u>Serve with:</u>
Sliced cucumbers, sliced radishes, celery sticks, carrot sticks, cauliflower florets
Cheese Crackers, Cream Cheese Crackers or *Saltine Crackers*
Gluten free crackers of your choice

Spinach and Artichoke Dip   **Category: A/C**   **Makes: 3 cups**

1-4 oz. can diced green chilies, drained
1-12 oz. jar artichoke hearts, drained and finely chopped
1-10 oz. package chopped frozen spinach, thawed and drained
1/2 cup sour cream
1/2 cup mayonnaise
2 to 3 cloves garlic, minced
1 cup Feta cheese or shredded Monterey Jack cheese
1/4 teaspoon pepper

Preheat oven to 400°.

Mix all ingredients together, reserving 1/3 cup of cheese for the topping.

Spread into a 9 inch oven proof casserole dish. Sprinkle with remaining cheese.

Bake for 20 minutes or until cheese is bubbling.

Serve with:
Gluten free tortilla chips or gluten free pita chips
Cheese Crackers, Cream Cheese Crackers or *Saltine Crackers*
Gluten free crackers of your choice

Bean Dip   **Category: B**   **Serves: 8-12**

1 tablespoon olive oil
1-15.5 oz. can black beans, drained
1-15.5 oz. can pinto beans, drained
1/2 medium onion, chopped
1/2 cup finely chopped roasted red pepper
1/3 cup fresh cilantro or parsley, chopped
2 cloves garlic, minced
1-4 oz. can green chilies, drained
2 tablespoons fresh lemon or lime juice
1 cup grated Cheddar cheese
1/2 cup *Fresh Salsa* (see page 63) or prepared salsa

Preheat oven to 350°.

In a skillet over medium heat, sauté onion and garlic in oil until tender, about 5 minutes. Add beans, red pepper, chilies and cilantro or parsley.

Cook for 5 minutes, stirring. Remove from heat stir in lemon or lime juice, cheese and salsa. Place in a food processor or blender until smooth.

Pour into a baking dish and bake for 5-10 minutes or until hot.

Serve with:
Gluten free tortilla chips or gluten free pita chips
Cheese Crackers, Cream Cheese Crackers or *Saltine Crackers*
Gluten free crackers of your choice

White Bean Dip with Garlic   **Category: B**   **Makes: 1 1/4 cups**

1-15 oz. can cannellini beans, drained
1 1/2 tablespoons fresh lemon juice
1 1/2 tablespoons extra-virgin olive oil
1 large garlic clove, peeled
3/4 teaspoon ground cumin
Salt and ground black pepper to taste
1 tablespoon chopped fresh mint
1 tablespoon chopped fresh dill
1 teaspoon grated lemon peel

Puree first 5 ingredients in food processor until almost smooth. Season with salt and pepper.

Transfer dip to small bowl. Mix mint, dill, and lemon peel in small dish; sprinkle over dip.

Serve with:
Gluten free tortilla chips or gluten free pita chips
Cheese Crackers, Cream Cheese Crackers or *Saltine Crackers*
Gluten free crackers of your choice

Spinach Balls   **Category: A/B**   **Makes: 2 - 3 dozen**

2-10 oz. packages frozen spinach, thawed and drained
1/2 cup onion, minced
2 cloves garlic, minced
1/2 cup Parmesan or Asiago cheese, shredded
1 cup cooked rice
3 eggs
2 tablespoons butter
1/8 teaspoon nutmeg
1/4 teaspoon salt
1/4 teaspoon pepper

Preheat oven to 350°. Lightly grease bottom of 13 by 9 inch baking pan.

Melt butter and let it cool slightly. Beat eggs in a bowl. Stir in onion, garlic, melted butter, spinach, rice, cheese, nutmeg, salt and pepper.

Form mixture into 1 1/2-inch balls and place in baking pan, leaving a small space between each.

Bake for 15-20 minutes or until lightly browned. Serve warm.

Hummus   Category: B   Makes: 3-1/2 cups

3 cloves garlic, minced
1/2 cup fresh parsley
2 green onions, sliced
2-15 oz. cans garbanzo beans (chick peas), drained and rinsed
6 tablespoons tahini (sesame spread)
1/2 teaspoon salt
1/2 teaspoon ground cumin
1/2 cup water, plus more if necessary
1-3 tablespoons fresh lemon juice (depending on your preference)

Place first 8 ingredients, and 1 tablespoon of the lemon juice in food processor or blender. Puree until smooth. Taste and add second and third tablespoons of lemon juice and/or additional salt, if desired.

If hummus seems too thick, stir in additional water 1 tablespoon at a time until desired consistency.

Serve with:
Sliced cucumbers, sliced radishes, celery sticks, carrot sticks, cauliflower florets
Cheese Crackers, Cream Cheese Crackers or *Saltine Crackers*
Gluten free crackers of your choice

Stuffed Mushrooms   **Category: A/C**   **Makes: 24**

24 whole large fresh mushrooms
1 cup cooked chopped crabmeat or shrimp
1 tablespoon fresh parsley (1 teaspoon dried)
1 teaspoon capers, drained and chopped
1 small onion, chopped
1 clove garlic, minced
2 tablespoons olive oil
Salt and ground black pepper to taste
1/4 cup Parmesan cheese or medium Cheddar cheese, shredded

Preheat oven to 350°. Lightly grease baking sheet.

Clean mushrooms and remove and discard the stems.

In a bowl, combine the seafood, capers, parsley, onion, garlic, oil, salt and pepper.

Fill each mushroom cap with one tablespoon of the mixture. Sprinkle cheese on top.

Arrange mushrooms on baking sheet so that they are not touching. Bake for 10-12 minutes or until the mushrooms are cooked through.

Cheddar Cheese Crackers   **Category: B**   **Makes: 5 dozen**

2/3 cup rice flour
1/4 teaspoon salt
1/2 teaspoon Xanthan gum
1/2 teaspoon baking powder
1/4 teaspoon baking soda
4 oz. sharp or extra sharp Cheddar cheese, shredded
4 tablespoons butter, softened
3 tablespoons milk
Salt
Dried herbs of choice (choose from dried basil, oregano, marjoram or rosemary)

Preheat oven to 400°.

Combine first 7 ingredients in a medium-sized bowl. Mix until the mixture resembles fine crumbs. Add the milk and beat well.

On a lightly greased surface, pat or roll the dough to 1/8-inch thickness. Cut into 3/4 inch squares.

Prick the tops of crackers with a fork and sprinkle lightly with salt and your choice of dried herbs.

Place on lightly greased baking sheet and bake until golden brown and crisp, 9-10 minutes.

The crackers will be light and crispy, although barely browning at the edges. The bottom of the crackers will have a bit more color.

Serve with:
Gluten free dips of your choice
Category A or B Soups
Category A or B Salads

Cream Cheese Crackers   **Category: B**   **Makes: 4 dozen**

2/3 cup potato starch or rice flour
1/4 teaspoon salt
1/4 teaspoon Xanthan gum
1/4 teaspoon baking soda
4 oz. cream cheese
4 tablespoons butter
1 tablespoon milk
Salt
Dried herbs of choice (choose from dried basil, oregano, marjoram or rosemary)

Preheat oven to 400°.

Combine first 6 ingredients in a medium size bowl. Mix until the mixture resembles fine crumbs. Add the milk and beat well.

By teaspoonfuls, roll the dough into balls and place on a lightly greased baking sheet. Press the dough flat with the heel of your hand. The crackers should be so thin that you can see the baking sheet through the dough.

Prick the tops of crackers with a fork and sprinkle lightly with salt and your choice of dried herbs.

Bake until golden brown and crisp, 6-8 minutes.

Serve with:
Gluten free dips of your choice
Category A or B Soups
Category A or B Salads

Saltine Crackers   **Category: B**   **Makes: 2 dozen**

2/3 cup rice flour
1/4 teaspoon salt
3/4 teaspoon Xanthan gum
1/4 teaspoon baking soda
1/2 teaspoon baking powder
6 tablespoons butter
1 egg white
1 teaspoon apple cider vinegar
1/4 cup plain yogurt
Salt

Preheat oven to 400°.

Combine the rice flour, salt, Xanthan gum, baking soda, baking powder and butter in a medium size bowl. Beat until the mixture forms fine crumbs. Add the remaining ingredients and beat well.

Press the dough as thinly as possible on an ungreased baking sheet, to 1/8 inch thickness or less. Moistened fingertips are helpful in pressing the dough. Cut into 1 1/2 inch squares.

Prick the tops of the crackers with a fork and sprinkle with salt.

Bake until golden brown and crisp, 10-12 minutes. The crackers will be light golden brown, with some spots a little darker. The crackers should not be soft or pliable but have a tender, crisp texture.

Serve with:
Gluten free dips of your choice
Category A or B Soups
Category A or B Salads

Crab Cocktail Spread   **Category: C**   **Makes: 2 cups**

1-8 oz. package cream cheese
1/2 cup cocktail sauce
1-7 1/2 oz. can white crabmeat

Place the softened cream cheese on a serving plate and drizzle the cocktail sauce over the cheese.
Gently place the crabmeat on top.

Serve with:
Sliced cucumbers, sliced radishes, celery sticks, cauliflower florets

Mini Veggie Quiches   **Category: C**   **Serves: 8**

Dough for one 9-inch *Pie Crust* (see page 217) or store bought gluten free pie crust, at room temperature
1 tablespoon canola oil
1/2 cup Artichoke hearts in water or fresh zucchini, diced (or 1/4 cup of each)
1 small diced fresh onion
1 tablespoon chopped fresh basil or 1 teaspoon dried basil
2 garlic cloves, minced
2 large eggs, at room temperature
1/2 cup heavy cream
1/4 teaspoon salt
2/3 cup Feta cheese
1 teaspoon chopped fresh parsley or 1/2 teaspoon dried parsley, for garnish

Preheat oven to 350°. Generously grease two mini-muffin pans (12 muffin cups each). Place rack in the bottom position of the oven.

With your fingers, press about 1/2 teaspoon of pie crust dough into each of the 24 muffin cups. Bake them for 5-7 minutes or until golden brown and set aside.

In a small skillet, heat the oil over medium heat. Add artichoke hearts and/or zucchini, onion, basil and garlic and cook, stirring constantly, until the vegetables become soft and translucent.

In a bowl, whisk eggs, cream, and salt together until smooth. Stir vegetable mixture into egg mixture until well blended. Fold in the feta cheese.

Divide mixture evenly among muffin cups, about a heaping tablespoon for each. Sprinkle with parsley.

Bake 15-20 minutes or until eggs are set. Remove from oven and serve immediately.

Spiced Nut Mix   **Category: C**   **Makes: 1 1/2 Cups**

1 teaspoon olive oil
1 teaspoon chili powder
1/4 teaspoon ground cumin
1/2 teaspoon garlic powder
1/2 teaspoon salt
2 cups shelled nuts, such as walnut halves, pecan halves, or almonds or a mixture of nuts of similar sizes

Preheat oven to 325°.

In a large bowl, stir together olive oil, chili powder, cumin, garlic powder and salt. Add nuts and toss until thoroughly and evenly coasted.

Arrange in a single layer on a large ungreased baking sheet.

Bake for 40 minutes, shaking pan occasionally to promote even browning.

Serve slightly warm.

 # Desserts

Most foods that people consider to be desserts contain mixtures of starches, proteins and sometimes fruit. As a result, they don't digest easily or comfortably. However, most people do like a sweet treat now and then. So for those people who "can't live without" desserts, most can eat them once in a while and still live completely free of stomach pain. Just remember that moderation is the key!

Ideally, all desserts should be eaten under the following guidelines:

1) Have dessert only on a rare or special occasion— for instance, a birthday, anniversary or holiday—once per month or less
2) Have a small serving or share it with someone—less is best
3) Wait as long as possible (preferably 3 hours or more) after a properly combined meal

Flan   **Category: Dessert**   **Serves: 6**

Ingredients:
1/2 cup sugar
2 cups heavy cream
1 teaspoon vanilla extract
3 eggs
1/4 cup sugar
1/2 cup blanched almonds (optional for garnish)
Sprig of mint (optional for garnish)
1 cup heavy cream, whipped (optional for garnish)

Required Equipment:
6 ramekins or one large baking dish (a pie plate or quiche dish is fine)
1 large 9 x 13 inch baking pan (for water bath)

Make sure ramekins are clean and dry.

Put a heavy skillet over medium heat for 30 seconds. Add 1/2 cup of sugar. With the back of the wooden spoon, keep sugar moving constantly in skillet until sugar is completely melted and has a rich, medium brown color (caramelized). Pour caramelized sugar into each of the 6 ramekins or large baking dish (whichever you are using); set aside.

Pour about 1/2 inch of warm water into the 9 x 13 inch baking dish, or boiling water if using ramekins. If using one large baking dish, be sure that the dish is tall enough to accommodate the water necessary.

Scald 2 cups of heavy cream in a saucepan. (Keep a close eye on the pan, so the cream does not boil over.)

Meanwhile in a mixing bowl, slightly beat 3 eggs. Mix in 1/4 cup sugar.

Stirring constantly, gradually add hot cream to egg mixture. Stir until the sugar is dissolved. Blend in 1 teaspoon vanilla extract. Ladle mixture into ramekins (or baking dish).

Place each of the ramekins (or baking dish) in the pan with water. If water level does not reach 3/4 of the way up the sides of the ramekins, carefully pour more water in. Bake uncovered in water bath at 325° for 50-60 minutes, or until a knife comes out clean when inserted half way between the center and edge of dish.

Note: To ensure custard does not over cook, check doneness after 45 minutes then every 5 minutes after.

Carefully remove each ramekin or baking dish from the water bath. Set on cooling rack until lukewarm, then chill flan thoroughly in the refrigerator, about 1 hour.

When ready to serve, un-mold by running a knife around the inside of the ramekin or baking dish. Place dessert plate on top of the ramekin or baking dish. With one hand under the ramekin or baking dish, and the other on top of the plate, turn over. Tap the ramekin or baking dish and the flan should drop onto the plate.

If it does not, carefully prod the flan out of the ramekin or dish with a small paring knife. It should slide out onto the plate.

Serve topped with almonds, mint and/or whipped cream if desired.

<u>Serve with:</u>
All desserts should be eaten either on an empty stomach or at least 3 hours after a properly combined meal.

Lemon Meringue Pie   **Category: Dessert**   **Serves: 8-10**

One 9-inch *Pie Crust* (see page 217) or store bought gluten free pie crust, unbaked

Filling:
1 cup sugar
5 tablespoons corn starch
1/4 teaspoon salt
1 cup water
1/2 cup milk
4 large egg yolks
1 tablespoon unsalted butter
1/2 cup fresh lemon juice
2 teaspoons freshly grated lemon zest

Meringue:
4 large egg whites
1/4 teaspoon cream of tartar
1/2 cup sugar
Pinch of salt

Preheat oven to 350°.

Filling: In a heavy sauce pan whisk together sugar, corn starch, and salt and gradually whisk in water and milk, whisking until corn starch is dissolved. Cook milk mixture over moderate heat, whisking until it comes to a boil.

In a bowl, whisk together egg yolks. Gradually whisk about 1/4 cup of hot milk mixture into yolks, then whisk yolk mixture into remaining milk mixture.

Simmer the mixture, whisking for 3 minutes. Remove pan from the heat and whisk in butter, lemon juice, and zest until the butter is melted. Cover the filling with plastic wrap to prevent a skin from forming.

Meringue: In a bowl with an electric mixer, beat egg whites with cream of tartar and a pinch of salt until they hold soft peaks. Beat in sugar, a little at a time until meringue just holds stiff peaks.
Pour filling into the shell and spread meringue on top, covering filling completely, sealing it to pastry. Draw meringue up into peaks with metal spatula or a knife and bake the pie in the middle of the oven until the meringue is golden; about 15 minutes.

Serve with:
All desserts should be eaten either on an empty stomach or at least 3 hours after a properly combined meal.

Pie Crust   **Category: Dessert**   **Makes: One 9 inch pie**

4 oz. cream cheese
2 tablespoons butter
2/3 cup rice flour
1 teaspoon sugar
1/2 teaspoon Xanthan gum
1/4 teaspoon baking powder

Combine all ingredients in a medium-size bowl. The mixture will first become a fine crumb, then finally a ball of dough.

Place the dough on a sheet of waxed paper or baking parchment. Cover with another sheet of paper and roll out into a large circle, about 12-13 inches in diameter.

Remove the top sheet and turn the dough upside down into a lightly greased 9 inch pie plate. Carefully remove the remaining sheet of paper.

Trim and pinch the dough at the edge of the pie rim by pinching the dough between your fingers. This will help the dough adhere to the pie plate so that there is no chance of the crust slipping into the plate while baking.

Prick the crust all over with a fork to stop air bubbles and slippage.

Fill with desired filling and bake as directed, or for a prepared crust, bake for 15-20 minutes at 400°, until golden. Let cool.

Flourless Chocolate Torte   **Category: Dessert**   **Serves: 6-8**

4-1 oz. squares semisweet chocolate, chopped
1/2 cup cocoa powder
1/2 cup butter
3/4 cup white sugar
3 eggs, beaten
1 teaspoon vanilla extract
1 cup heavy cream, whipped

Preheat oven to 300°. Grease an 8 inch round cake pan, and dust lightly with extra cocoa powder.

In the top of a double boiler over lightly simmering water, melt chopped chocolate and butter. Remove from heat and stir in sugar, cocoa powder, eggs, and vanilla. Pour this mixture into previously prepared pan.

Bake in the oven for 30 minutes. Let the torte cool in pan for 10 minutes then turn out onto a wire rack to cool completely.

Serve topped with whipped cream.

<u>Serve with:</u>
All desserts should be eaten either on an empty stomach or at least 3 hours after a properly combined meal.

Banana Pudding   **Category: Dessert**   **Serves: 6-8**

5 large egg yolks
1/4 cup corn starch
1/2 cup plus 2 teaspoons sugar
1/4 teaspoon salt
2 cups whole milk
3 tablespoons banana liqueur (optional)
2 tablespoons cold unsalted butter plus 1 tablespoon melted butter
2 teaspoons pure vanilla extract
1 cup coarsely ground *Shortbread Cookies* (see page 234) or store bought gluten free shortbread cookies
1/4 teaspoon cinnamon
2 bananas, coarsely chopped

In a bowl, whisk the egg yolks with the corn starch, 1/2 cup of the sugar and salt.

In a medium sauce pan, bring the milk to a boil. Gradually whisk the milk into the egg yolks until smooth. Transfer the pudding mixture into the sauce pan and add the banana liqueur. Cook over moderate heat, whisking, until the pudding is thick; about 3 minutes.

Scrape the pudding into a bowl and whisk in the cold butter and vanilla. Cover with plastic wrap and refrigerate for about 4 hours.

Preheat the oven to 325°. Line a baking sheet with parchment paper. In a bowl, combine the cookies, cinnamon, the remaining 2 teaspoons of sugar and a pinch of salt. Stir in the melted butter. Spread the mixture on the prepared baking sheet; bake for 15 minutes, until lightly browned. Let it cool.

Spoon the chopped bananas into bowls, cover with the pudding, and sprinkle with the crumb mix. Serve right away.

Serve with:
All desserts should be eaten either on an empty stomach or at least 3 hours after a properly combined meal.

Double Chocolate Pudding   **Category: Dessert**   **Serves: 6-8**

2 tablespoons Dutch-processed cocoa
2 tablespoons corn starch
2/3 cup sugar
1/8 teaspoon salt
1 cup light cream
3 large egg yolks
2 cups whole milk
6 oz. bittersweet or semisweet chocolate, melted and cooled slightly
1 tablespoon unsalted butter, softened
2 teaspoons vanilla extract
1 cup heavy cream, whipped

Sift the cocoa, corn starch, sugar, and salt into a medium, heavy bottom sauce pan. Slowly whisk the light cream, followed by the yolks, then the milk. Stir in the chocolate. The chocolate will form clumps that will smooth through cooking.

Bring the mixture to a boil over medium-high heat, stirring constantly with a whisk and scraping the bottom and sides of the saucepan. The pudding will gradually darken and thicken. Reduce the heat to medium and cook, stirring gently but constantly with a wooden spoon, until the pudding coats the spoon very thickly; about 1 1/2 to 2 minutes.

Pass the pudding through a fine-mesh strainer to a medium bowl, pressing it through with a rubber spatula. Stir in the butter and vanilla. Cover with plastic wrap, pressing it directly on to the pudding surface and refrigerate until cool and set; at least 3 hours or up to 2 days.

Spoon the pudding into serving dishes and top with whipped cream.

Serve with:
All desserts should be eaten either on an empty stomach or at least 3 hours after a properly combined meal.

Chocolate Mousse   **Category: Dessert**   **Serves: 6-8**

6 oz. bittersweet or semisweet chocolate, chopped coarse
4 tablespoons unsalted butter
Pinch of salt
1 teaspoon vanilla extract
2 tablespoons strong coffee or 4 tablespoons brandy, orange liqueur, or light rum
4 large eggs, separated
2 tablespoons sugar
1/2 cup chilled heavy cream, plus more for serving

Melt the chocolate in a medium bowl set over barely simmering water, stirring once at the 2 minute mark. Whisk the butter into the melted chocolate, 1 tablespoon at a time. Stir in the salt, vanilla, and coffee until completely incorporated. Whisk in the yolks, one at a time, making sure that each is fully incorporated before adding the next; set the mixture aside.

Stir the egg whites in a clean mixing bowl set over a sauce pan of hot water until slightly warm; about 1-2 minutes. Remove the bowl from the sauce pan. Beat with an electric mixer set at medium speed until soft peaks form. Raise the mixer speed to high and slowly add the sugar; beat into soft peaks. Whisk a quarter of the beaten whites into the chocolate mixture, then gently fold in the remaining whites.

Whip the cream to soft peaks. Gently fold the whipped cream into the mousse. Spoon into 6-8 individual serving dishes. Cover and refrigerate for at least two hours. (The mousse may be covered and refrigerated for up to 24 hours.) Serve with additional whipped cream.

Serve with:
All desserts should be eaten either on an empty stomach or at least 3 hours after a properly combined meal.

White Cake   **Category: Dessert**   **Serves: 8-10**

2/3 cup white rice flour
1/2 cup tapioca starch
1/3 cup corn starch
3/4 teaspoon Xanthan gum
1 1/2 teaspoons gluten free baking powder
1/2 teaspoon salt
1/2 cup shortening or butter, softened
3/4 cup granulated sugar
3 eggs
3/4 teaspoon vanilla extract
1 teaspoon apple cider vinegar
1/2 cup milk

Preheat oven to 350°. Lightly grease an 8 inch square baking pan.

In a large bowl, sift rice flour, tapioca starch, corn starch, Xanthan gum, baking powder and salt.

In a separate bowl, cream shortening or butter and sugar until light and fluffy. Add eggs, one at a time, beating well after each addition. Stir in vanilla extract and vinegar. Stir in dry ingredients alternately with milk, making three additions of dry ingredients and two of milk. Stir just until combined after each addition.

Spoon into prepared pan. Spread to edges and smooth top with a moist rubber spatula. Let stand for 30 minutes. Bake in preheated oven for 35-40 minutes or until a toothpick inserted in the center comes out clean. Let cool in the pan on a rack for 10 minutes. Remove from the pan and let cool completely on rack.

Frost with *Chocolate Glaze* (see page 226), your favorite icing or dust with confectioner's sugar if desired.

Serve with:
All desserts should be eaten either on an empty stomach or at least 3 hours after a properly combined meal.

Chocolate Fudge Cake　　　　**Category: Dessert**　　　　**Serves: 8-10**

3/4 cup whole bean flour
3/4 cup sorghum flour
1/2 cup potato starch
1/4 cup tapioca starch
1 teaspoon Xanthan gum
1/2 teaspoon gluten free baking powder
1 1/2 teaspoons baking soda
1/2 teaspoon salt
3/4 cup unsweetened cocoa powder
3/4 cup shortening or butter, softened
1 1/2 cups packed brown sugar
3 eggs
2 teaspoons vanilla extract
2 cups sour cream

Preheat oven to 350°. Lightly grease two 8 inch round pans.

In a large bowl, sift together whole bean flour, sorghum flour, potato starch, tapioca starch, Xanthan gum, baking powder, baking soda, salt and cocoa.

In a separate bowl, cream shortening and brown sugar until light and fluffy. Add eggs, one at a time, beating well after each addition. Stir in vanilla extract. Stir in dry ingredients alternately with sour cream to shortening-sugar mixture, making three additions of dry ingredients and two of sour cream.

Spoon into prepared pans. Spread to edges and smooth tops with a moist rubber spatula. Let stand for 30 minutes. Bake in preheated oven for 35 to 40 minutes or until a toothpick inserted in the center comes out clean. Let cool in the pan on a rack for 10 minutes. Remove from the pans and let cool completely on racks.

Frost with *Chocolate Glaze* (see page 226), your favorite icing or dust with confectioner's sugar if desired.

<u>Serve with:</u>
All desserts should be eaten either on an empty stomach or at least 3 hours after a properly combined meal.

Cheesecake   **Category: Dessert**   **Serves: 8-10**

Base:
1/4 cup melted butter
1/4 cup packed brown sugar
3 cups *White Cake* crumbs (see page 222)

Cheesecake:
2-8 oz. packages cream cheese, softened
1 cup granulated sugar
2 tablespoons corn starch
1 teaspoon freshly squeezed lemon juice
4 eggs
1 cup milk

Preheat oven to 350°. Lightly grease 10-inch springform pan.

In a large bowl, combine butter, brown sugar and cake crumbs. Mix well. Press into prepared pan. Set aside.

In a large bowl, beat the cream cheese until smooth. Slowly add sugar, corn starch and lemon juice. Beat until light and fluffy. Add egg, one at a time, beating well after each. Mix in milk. Pour into prepared pan.

Bake in preheated oven for 45-55 minutes or until the center is just set. Let cool in oven for 30 minutes with the oven turned off. Remove from the oven and continue to cool in pan on a rack for another 30 minutes. Refrigerate until chilled, about 3 hours.

Serve with:
All desserts should be eaten either on an empty stomach or at least 3 hours after a properly combined meal.

Chocolate Glaze   **Category: Dessert**   **Makes: 1 Cup**

1/2 cup unsweetened cocoa powder
2 tablespoons granulated sugar
2 tablespoons corn starch
1/3 cup milk
1/4 cup corn syrup
1 teaspoon vanilla extract

In a small saucepan, sift together cocoa, sugar and corn starch. Whisk in milk, corn syrup and vanilla extract. Bring to a boil over medium heat, stirring constantly, until glaze boils. Boil for 1-2 minutes until thickened and glossy. Cool 5 minutes.

Drizzle over cooled cake.

Serve with:
All desserts should be eaten either on an empty stomach or at least 3 hours after a properly combined meal.

Fudgy Brownies   **Category: Dessert**   **Makes: 16**

1/3 cup whole bean flour
2 tablespoons potato starch
1 cup packed brown sugar
1/2 teaspoon gluten free baking powder
1/2 teaspoon Xanthan gum
1/8 teaspoon salt
1/2 cup chopped walnuts
1/2 cup shortening
2 oz. unsweetened chocolate
1/2 teaspoon vanilla extract
2 eggs

Preheat oven to 350°. Lightly grease an 8 inch square baking pan.

In a large bowl or plastic bag, combine whole bean flour, potato starch, brown sugar, baking powder, Xanthan gum, salt and walnuts. Mix well and set aside.

In a large bowl, microwave shortening and chocolate on Medium for 3 minutes or until partially melted (or heat in a saucepan over hot water until partially melted). Stir until melted. Add eggs, one at a time, blending after each. Stir in vanilla extract.

Slowly add dry ingredients, stirring until combined. Spread evenly in prepared pan. Let stand for 30 minutes.

Bake in a preheated oven for 20-25 minutes or until a toothpick inserted in the center still has a little moist crumb adhering to it. Transfer to a rack to cool completely. Let cool for 15 minutes on rack.

<u>Serve with:</u>
All desserts should be eaten either on an empty stomach or at least 3 hours after a properly combined meal.

Toffee Blondies   **Category: Dessert**   **Makes: 1 1/2 Dozen**

3/4 cup brown rice flour
1/2 cup whole bean flour
1/4 cup tapioca starch
2 teaspoons gluten free baking powder
2 teaspoons Xanthan gum
1/4 teaspoon salt
1/2 cup butter, softened
3/4 cup granulated sugar
1/3 cup packed brown sugar
2 eggs
1 teaspoon vanilla extract
1/2 cup toffee bits
1/2 cup white chocolate chips

Preheat oven to 350°. Lightly grease a 13 x 9 inch baking pan.

In a large bowl, sift together brown rice flour, whole bean flour, tapioca starch, baking powder, Xanthan gum and salt. Resift and set aside.

In a separate bowl, cream butter, granulated sugar and brown sugar. Add eggs and vanilla extract. Beat until light and fluffy. Gradually beat in dry ingredients, mixing just until smooth. Stir in toffee bits and white chocolate chips.

Spoon into prepared pan, spread to edges and smooth top. Let stand for 30 minutes.

Bake in preheated oven for 35 to 45 minutes or until a toothpick inserted in the center comes out clean. Transfer to cooling rack and let cool completely. Cut into bars.

Serve with:
All desserts should be eaten either on an empty stomach or at least 3 hours after a properly combined meal.

Cinnamon Pecan Squares   **Category: Dessert**   **Makes: 2 Dozen**

1 2/3 cups soy flour
1/3 cup tapioca starch
1/2 teaspoon baking soda
1 teaspoon Xanthan gum
1/4 teaspoon salt
1 tablespoon ground cinnamon
1 cup butter, softened
1/2 cup packed brown sugar
1/2 cup granulated sugar
1 egg, separated
1 cup chopped pecans

Preheat oven to 300°. Lightly grease a 10 by 10 inch baking pan.

In a bowl or plastic bag, combine soy flour, tapioca starch, baking soda, Xanthan gum, salt and cinnamon. Mix well and set aside.

In a separate bowl, cream butter, brown sugar, granulated sugar and egg yolk until light and fluffy. Slowly beat in the dry ingredients until combined.

Form the dough into a large disk and place in the prepared pan. Firmly pat down the dough to fit the pan.

In a small bowl, beat egg white with a fork just until foamy. Brush on top of the dough. Sprinkle with pecans and press them in lightly. Let stand for 30 minutes.

Bake in preheated oven for 35-45 minutes or until set. Immediately cut into bars. Finish cooling in the pan.

<u>Serve with:</u>
All desserts should be eaten either on an empty stomach or at least 3 hours after a properly combined meal.

Chocolate Covered Peanut Bars   **Category: Dessert**   **Makes: 16**

3/4 cup soy flour
1/3 cup whole bean flour
2 tablespoons tapioca starch
1 1/2 teaspoons Xanthan gum
1 tablespoon gluten free baking powder
1/2 cup butter or shortening, softened
1/2 cup gluten free peanut butter
2/3 cup packed brown sugar
3 eggs
2 teaspoons vanilla
1 cup chopped peanuts
1 cup chocolate chips

Preheat oven to 325°. Lightly grease 9 inch baking pan.

In a small bowl or plastic bag, combine soy flour, whole bean flour, tapioca starch, Xanthan gum and baking powder. Mix well and set aside

In a large bowl, cream butter, peanut butter and brown sugar until well blended. Add eggs and vanilla and cream until light and fluffy. Slowly beat in the dry ingredients until combined. Stir in peanuts.

Spoon into prepared pan. Using a moistened rubber spatula, spread to edges and smooth top. Sprinkle with chocolate chips. Let stand for 30 minutes.

Bake in preheated oven 30-35 minutes, or until a toothpick inserted in the center comes out clean. Spread melted chocolate chips to evenly cover the top. Let cool completely on a rack. Cut into bars.

Serve with:
All desserts should be eaten either on an empty stomach or at least 3 hours after a properly combined meal.

Peanut Butter Cookies   **Category: Dessert**   **Makes: 3 Dozen**

1 cup soy flour
1/2 cup packed brown sugar
1/2 cup granulated sugar
1/3 cup corn starch
1/2 teaspoon baking soda
1/2 teaspoon Xanthan gum
1/4 teaspoon salt
1/2 cup butter, softened
1/2 cup gluten free peanut butter
1 egg
1/2 teaspoon vanilla extract

Preheat oven to 350°.

In a bowl or plastic bag, combine soy flour, brown sugar, granulated sugar, corn starch, baking soda, Xanthan gum and salt. Mix well and set aside.

In a separate bowl, cream butter and peanut butter. Add egg and vanilla. Beat until light and fluffy. Slowly stir in the dry ingredients until combined. With a rubber spatula, scrape the bottom and sides of bowl.

Gather the dough into a large ball, kneading in any remaining dry ingredients. Roll into 1-inch balls. Place 1 1/2 inches apart on ungreased baking sheets. Flatten slightly with a fork.

Bake in preheated oven for 10-15 minutes or until set. Transfer to a cooling rack immediately.

<u>Serve with:</u>
All desserts should be eaten either on an empty stomach or at least 3 hours after a properly combined meal.

Chocolate Chip Cookies   **Category: Dessert**   **Makes: 6 Dozen**

1 cup sorghum flour
2/3 cup whole bean flour
1/2 cup tapioca starch
1 teaspoon baking soda
1 teaspoon Xanthan gum
1/2 teaspoon salt
1 cup shortening, softened
1 1/3 cups packed brown sugar
2 eggs
1 teaspoon vanilla extract
2 cups mini-chocolate chips
1 cup chopped walnuts

Preheat oven to 350°.

In a bowl or plastic bag, combine sorghum flour, whole bean flour, tapioca starch, baking soda, Xanthan gum and salt. Mix well and set aside.

In a separate bowl, cream shortening and brown sugar.   Add eggs and vanilla extract and beat until light and fluffy. Slowly beat in the dry ingredients until combined. Stir in chocolate chips and walnuts.

Drop dough by level teaspoonfuls, 1 1/2 inches apart onto lightly greased baking sheets. Let stand for 30 minutes.

Bake in preheated oven for 8-10 minutes or until set. Remove from baking sheets to a cooling rack immediately.

Serve with:
All desserts should be eaten either on an empty stomach or at least 3 hours after a properly combined meal.

Mocha Chocolate Cookies   **Category: Dessert**   **Makes: 5 Dozen**

1 cup sorghum flour
2/3 cup whole bean flour
1/2 cup tapioca starch
1 teaspoon baking soda
1 teaspoon Xanthan gum
1/2 teaspoon salt
1/3 cup unsweetened cocoa powder, sifted
4 oz. semi-sweet chocolate
1/3 cup butter
1/3 cup shortening
2 tablespoons water
1 tablespoon instant coffee granules
2 eggs
2/3 cup granulated sugar
2/3 cup packed brown sugar
1 1/2 teaspoons vanilla
1 cup semi-sweet chocolate chips

Preheat oven to 350°. In a large bowl or plastic bag, combine sorghum flour, whole bean flour, tapioca starch, baking soda, Xanthan gum, salt and cocoa. Mix well and set aside.

In a medium microwave-safe bowl, microwave chocolate, butter, shortening, water and coffee granules, uncovered, on Medium-low (40% power) for 2 minutes. Stir until completely melted. Set aside to cool.

In a large bowl, beat eggs, sugar and brown sugar for 3 minutes, until smooth. Add vanilla and cooled melted chocolate mixture. Slowly beat in the dry ingredients until combined. Stir in chocolate chips. Drop dough by rounded spoonfuls 2 inches apart on lightly greased baking sheets. Let stand for 30 minutes. Bake for 10-12 minutes, or until set. Transfer to a cooling rack immediately.

Serve with:
All desserts should be eaten either on an empty stomach or at least 3 hours after a properly combined meal.

Shortbread Cookies   **Category: Dessert**   **Makes: 2 Dozen**

2/3 cup rice flour
1/2 cup corn starch
1/2 cup sifted gluten free confectioner's sugar
1/4 cup potato starch
2 tablespoons tapioca starch
3/4 cup butter, softened
Sweet rice flour to flatten (if needed)

Preheat oven to 300°.

In a bowl or plastic bag, combine rice flour, corn starch, confectioner's sugar, potato starch and tapioca starch. Mix well and set aside.

In a separate bowl, cream butter. Slowly beat in the dry ingredients until combined. With a rubber spatula, scrape the bottom and sides of bowl.

Gather the dough into a large ball, kneading in any remaining dry ingredients. Roll into 1-inch balls. Place 1 inch apart on baking sheets. If desired, flatten with fork dipped into sweet rice flour.

Bake in preheated oven for 15-25 minutes or until set but not browned. Transfer to a cooling rack immediately.

Serve with:
All desserts should be eaten either on an empty stomach or at least 3 hours after a properly combined meal.

Creamy Rice Pudding   **Category: Dessert**   **Serves: 4**

2 cups milk
1/3 cup rice
3 tablespoons sugar
2 teaspoons butter
Pinch of salt
1/2 teaspoon vanilla extract
1/4 teaspoon ground nutmeg
1/3 cup raisins

In a large saucepan over medium heat, combine milk, rice, sugar, butter and salt. Heat, stirring often, until tiny bubbles form around the edge. Reduce heat to low. Cover and simmer, stirring occasionally, for 1 hour or until rice is tender.

Remove from heat. Stir in vanilla, nutmeg and raisins. Serve warm or chilled.

Serve with:
All desserts should be eaten either on an empty stomach or at least 3 hours after a properly combined meal.

Index--Alphabetical

C

D

Index—By Category

Category--Beverage

Category C--Proteins

Category--Condiments

Category--Desserts

Category--Fruit